TWO MINUTES
IN THE **BIBLE**™

THROUGH

Psalms

BOYD BAILEY

HARVEST HOUSE PUBLISHERS
EUGENE, OREGON

Cover by Left Coast Design, Portland, Oregon

Cover Photo © Creative Travel Projects / Shutterstock

TWO MINUTES IN THE BIBLE is a trademark of Boyd Bailey. Harvest House Publishers, Inc., is the exclusive licensee of the trademark TWO MINUTES IN THE BIBLE.

TWO MINUTES IN THE BIBLE™ THROUGH PSALMS

Copyright © 2016 Boyd Bailey
Published by Harvest House Publishers
Eugene, Oregon 97402
www.harvesthousepublishers.com

ISBN 978-0-7369-6577-4 (pbk.)
ISBN 978-0-7369-6578-1 (eBook)

Library of Congress Cataloging-in-Publication Data
Names: Bailey, Boyd, 1960- author.
Title: Two minutes in the Bible through Psalms / Boyd Bailey.
Description: Eugene, Oregon : Harvest House Publishers, 2016.
Identifiers: LCCN 2015044107 (print) | LCCN 2016016428 (ebook) | ISBN 9780736965774 (pbk.) | ISBN 9780736965781 (eBook)
Subjects: LCSH: Bible. Psalms—Devotional literature.
Classification: LCC BS1430.54 .B34 2016 (print) | LCC BS1430.54 (ebook) | DDC 242/.5—dc23
LC record available at https://lccn.loc.gov/2015044107

Printed in the United States of America

16 17 18 19 20 21 22 23 24 / BP-SK / 10 9 8 7 6 5 4 3 2 1

To our four daughters,
Rebekah, Rachel, Bethany, and Anna,
whose King is enthralled by their beauty.

Psalm 45:11

Acknowledgments

Thank you, Pete and Debbie Ochs, for your generosity that made this book possible.

Thank you, Billy Graham, for modeling a life that daily drinks from the psalms.

Thank you, Susan Fox and Gene Skinner, for your expert editing.

Thank you, Wisdom Hunters Board of Directors, for your love, prayers, and accountability.

Thank you, Gwynne Maffett, for being our Wisdom Hunters prayer warrior.

Thank you, Bob Hawkins and Harvest House Publishers, for your vision and support for this book.

Introduction

The psalms are my default to experience God in all His glory. They describe the Lord as a secure refuge, a cool place to rest under the shadow of His wing. Righteous refreshment is found in God's green grass beside still waters—care from our loving Great Shepherd for His sheep. Sound security accompanies a trusting soul.

The psalms invite peace and reveal pain. The 150 chapters of truth and transparency communicate trust in the Lord and struggle with sin and distrust. Some seeking souls are tortured by fear and doubt, while others are quieted under the calming hand of Christ. Fortunately, faith eventually wins out for most—though getting there isn't always easy!

Most of the psalms flow from the lives of people who are seeking the Lord. David, Moses, and the other psalmists describe their unique experiences with God. They are so intensely personal that you feel their emotion gradually bubble up from hurt and anger or immediately explode into praise and adoration. These writings are raw and real—at times I bow my head and pray a psalm because it helps me bare my heart.

The psalms can be described as songs, hymns, canticles, poems, and prayers. Out of these diverse writing styles, tantalizing truths wait to capture a willing heart. We often live to meet our felt needs, but when we meditate on a psalm with a humble heart, we experience something better—a deeper level of intimacy with the Lord.

Do you question the existence of God? Do you sometimes wonder why good people suffer and bad people prosper? Have crushing circumstances made you mad at yourself, at God, and at others? Or are you at the pinnacle of pleasure and success—and tempted to take the credit? Are you in need of fresh soul-care in rest, reflection, praise, and worship?

Regardless of where you find yourself on the continuum of following Christ, you can engage with eternity in the psalms. Perhaps you once burned with passion for God, but life has gradually lessened your enthusiasm for godly living. The psalms are a reliable remedy to reignite your fiery faith. Has adversity beat up your emotions and left you feeling alone? Your heavenly Father will meet you through these love letters.

At times my doubts drive me to my knees with the book of Psalms open before me. I read and pray over each word and phrase, searching for a divine antidote for my fears. And then, just as the Rosetta Stone interprets ancient Egyptian hieroglyphics, the Holy Spirit reads God's purpose for my life into my willing heart. He uses His Word to comfort and convict my heart and to instruct my head. I forget, but He lovingly reminds.

These simple writings will help you focus your attention on the Lord and open your heart to His love. They're not ends in themselves, but rather starting points of where God wants to take you in your faith walk. Confess your need for Him, and He will not disappoint you.

"Teach me your way, LORD, that I may rely on your faithfulness; give me an undivided heart, that I may fear your name" (Psalm 86:11).

A fellow servant and friend of Jesus,

Boyd Bailey
Roswell, GA

1

Refuge in Him

Blessed are all who take refuge in him.

PSALM 2:12

Outside of Christ, we are refugees in need of a refuge. Our soul seeks asylum in Almighty God. Our spirit is on a search for security and peace. Deep within our innermost desires, we want refuge in God. Otherwise we wander around earth untethered to truth. Away from heaven we're refugees. We need a secure place, and Jesus is our sanctuary.

Even if your faith is as slender as a spider's thread, you can still trust in Jesus. The object of your faith matters more than the amount of your faith. His refuge isn't just for the robust of faith—it's especially available to those of us flailing away in doubt and fear. We've lost our way, and we need wisdom to map out our faith. When we take refuge in Him, we're blessed with clarity and conviction. The Spirit is our shelter.

"I will say of the LORD, 'He is my refuge and my fortress,
my God, in whom I trust'" (Psalm 91:2).

He's our refuge when hope seems extinct. He's our refuge when financial obligations are ravishing our resources. He's our refuge when people we depend on are nowhere to be found. He's our refuge when health issues weigh us down. He's our refuge when fear tests our courage. He's our refuge when our marriage hangs in the balance. He's our refuge when work pressures pulsate in our mind and awaken us at night. He's our refuge when all seems to be going wrong. He's our refuge when all seems to be going right. God is our refuge.

We're blessed when we find refuge with our Creator. The Almighty supplies us with wisdom and understanding when we take time to listen to His instruction. Our prayers over His Word open our hearts to illuminating insights. The place of refuge holds up truth and casts out lies. Stability is another blessing from resting in His refuge. Our world rocks around us, but we have a rock in our Lord. He's not a suspension bridge that sways with the winds of the world's unpredictability. Nothing about our Savior is shaky.

—∞∞∞—

"The LORD is good,
a refuge in times of trouble.
He cares for those who trust in him" (Nahum 1:7).

How can I take refuge in God and His loving-kindness? What results from resting in Him?

Related Readings
Exodus 33:22; Psalm 46:1-3; Isaiah 25:4; Jeremiah 16:19

2

Peace of Mind

_I lie down and sleep;
I wake again, because the LORD sustains me.
I will not fear though tens of thousands
assail me on every side._

PSALM 3:5-6

P eace of mind comes from our Master Jesus. He masterfully puts our mind at ease with His eternal perspective. Trust in Him gives us tranquil thoughts. Without His peace, we worry and fret. A mind without peace is paralyzed by the thought of everything going awry. What _can_ go wrong _will_ go wrong because the odds are stacked against us. Without the peace of Christ, we find ourselves with an overwhelming sense of dread, even despair. In Christ we have peace.

Jesus isn't stingy with His peace. He gives it liberally and lovingly.

Beware of the fleeting peace the world offers. It's a cheap substitute. The world's peace is circumstantial. God's peace transcends circumstances. The world's peace is temporal. His peace is eternal. The world's peace leads you away from God and reality. His peace leads you to engage with both. The world's peace produces a limited perspective. His peace results in a view of life that's robust and real. The world's peace cannot remove fear. His peace overcomes fear with faith.

_"Peace I leave with you; my peace
I give you" (John 14:27)._

Once you apply the peace of Christ, you have peace of mind. Peace of mind gives you a platform for living purposefully. Because you live with purpose and peace, you garner influence with others. People are attracted to the peaceful. They want to learn how to find peace and apply it to their life circumstances.

Your friends or family may not acknowledge it, but your peace is proof of God's existence. Peace is a powerful apologetic for the Almighty. Your calmness during crisis can only be explained by Christ. Because you lean on Him, others want to lean on you.

Use your peace of mind as a gauge for God's will. If you have peace, proceed; if you lack peace, be cautious. God's peace is a green light to go forward. The absence of His peace is a red light to refrain. Therefore be sensitive to the Spirit's peaceful prodding to go or stay. Either way you're okay as long as the Lord's peace is preeminent. Peace calms your mind and enables you to think clearly. Peace positions you for wise thinking.

"The peace of God, which transcends all understanding, will guard your hearts and your minds in Christ Jesus" (Philippians 4:7).

Why does Jesus want me to access His peace? How does His peace guard my heart and mind?

Related Readings
Isaiah 26:3; John 16:33; Romans 16:20; Ephesians 3:19

3

Chosen by God

———— ⟨∞⟩ ————

Know that the LORD has set apart his
faithful servant for himself;
the LORD hears when I call to him.

PSALM 4:3

God chooses His children for Himself. Our relationship with our Lord is all about Him. It's all about His desires, His pleasures, His vision, His goals, His will. When we came to God, we came empty-handed, clinging only to the cross of Christ. In our surrender to our Savior we emptied ourselves and received Jesus. We went from self-sufficient to God-dependent. We went from ungodly to godly. We went from an impersonal relationship with a distant God to an intimate relationship with our heavenly Father. God chose us for Himself.

The Lord wants you to know and follow His heart. He owns your life. You may be struggling with traveling overseas for the sake of His cause, although Jesus clearly commands us to go into all the world and make disciples. Or you may be too busy to build a relationship with your neighbors. But your sensitive Savior implores you to love those around you. You're at His disposal to carry out His desires.

———— ⟨∞⟩ ————

"Love the LORD, all his faithful people!
The LORD preserves those who are true to him,
but the proud he pays back in full" (Psalm 31:23).

God offers a clear channel of communication for His children. He hears when we call to Him. Prayer isn't passive for our heavenly Father. He's interested in our intense circumstances and our heartfelt fears. He listens to and answers our prayers. It's not always the answer we think we need. Whether He answers yes or no, He defines His will for us. We have no need to fear, for our heavenly Father is near.

The more we constantly converse with Christ, the more boldly we'll speak to people. Prayer is a purging and a preparation. It's God's platform to launch us into fields that are ripe for harvest. It's a preparation for engagement in the lives of people. Prayer fills us with love so we can be emptied of love. We're chosen by God. What He chooses He makes holy. Without holiness we cannot see our Savior. Because He was poured out, we are sold out!

What does it mean to be set apart for the Lord? How does God preserve His people?

Related Readings
Psalm 18:25; Micah 7:7; 1 Timothy 4:7; Revelation 2:10

4

Troublemakers

———— ◦◦◦ ————

The trouble they cause recoils on them;
their violence comes down on their own heads.

PSALM 7:16

Troublemakers tend to self-destruct. There's no need to get worked up over their acts of deception. They're dishonest. They lie when the truth will suffice. The harm they intend to inflict on others comes back to hurt them. Troublemakers attempt to discredit those they're jealous of and in the process discredit themselves. Troublemakers conceive elaborate plans with evil intent. It's all about them and their agenda. They can easily tell you one thing and do another. In their mind the desired outcome justifies the polluted process.

Beware of troublemakers, but don't urge them on with too much attention. Keep an eye on them, but don't be consumed by them. Stand up to them in the right spirit without crushing their spirit. They're totally insecure and fearful but afraid to admit their insecurities. Because their acceptance is based on performance, they're always looking for ways to impress others.

It's not what we do that keeps us secure; it's who we are and whose we are. In Christ we have all we need.

———— ◦◦◦ ————

"As I have observed, those who plow evil
and those who sow trouble reap it" (Job 4:8).

Trust God with troublemakers. You're not their judge and jury. He will handle them in His timing and in His way. We have our own sins to confess and repent of on a regular basis. Our sins may not be as blatant, but they're still present. We may not sin in such a pronounced manner as a troublemaker; nonetheless we still struggle with dishonesty and deception. It may be on a smaller scale, but we still weigh in as one who struggles with being a troublemaker.

So let's contrast the life of a troublemaker by being a blessing maker. Let's be a blessing instead of a curse. Let's extend consolation instead of consternation. Let's focus on giving instead of taking. Let's be a solace instead of a pain. Let's serve instead of being served. Let's encourage instead of discourage. Kill them with kindness, and watch God turn their hearts toward Him. Give them the respect they never had, and they may begin to respect themselves. God's grace can change troublemakers into blessing makers. We are proof!

"He lifted me out of the slimy pit,
out of the mud and mire;
he set my feet on a rock
and gave me a firm place to stand" (Psalm 40:2).

How can I become more of a peacemaker? How can I love troublemakers?

Related Readings
Psalms 9:15; 35:7-8; Proverbs 11:18; 26:27; Hosea 8:7; Galatians 6:7-8

5

Lips of Children

⸻ ∞ ⸻

Through the praise of children and infants
you have established a stronghold against your enemies,
to silence the foe and the avenger.

PSALM 8:2

The lips of children lift up the greatness of God in praise and adoration. Children don't know any better than to believe God and take Him at His word. They are trusting and pure in their devotion. In Christ's triumphant entry into Jerusalem, children embraced His coronation. They shouted "Hosanna in the highest." Humility praises Jesus, but pride is silent. Humility invites Jesus, but pride is threatened by Jesus. Humility wants to sit in His lap, but pride rejects His affection.

Children live in a constant state of dependence. They depend on their parents for food, clothing, and shelter. Children look to their parents to teach them about God and religion. Parents are a plethora of resources for their children. Boys and girls depend on Mom and Dad for understanding what they do well and how they can best excel. Parents are a warehouse of wisdom for their offspring. Wise children learn from and depend on their parents. They're dependent.

⸻ ∞ ⸻

"Truly I tell you, unless you change and become
like little children, you will never enter the
kingdom of heaven" (Matthew 18:3).

Our relationship with God is no different. We're His children in desperate need of His direction. We may spurn His discipline at times, but we come back because we know He's what we need. We need His wisdom. We need His forgiveness. We need His comfort, love, and hope. We need His patience to work effectively with people. We need His security found in Christ. We need His courage in crisis. We need His grace in the middle of criticism. We need His humility to defeat our pride.

Children are the conscience of adults. They remind us of our dependence on Jesus. We're but a grain of sand on the seashore of humanity. Jesus is Lord of all, and we serve and worship Him alone. The lips of children naturally lift up the glory of God. And we do so supernaturally by the Holy Spirit's power. We cannot keep quiet because of His lavish love and abundant grace. It's in our childlike faith that God reveals Himself. We're God's child; therefore we praise Him!

"Jesus, full of joy through the Holy Spirit, said, 'I praise you, Father, Lord of heaven and earth, because you have hidden these things from the wise and learned, and revealed them to little children'" (Luke 10:21).

What is childlike faith? Why is childlike faith required for daily trust in God?

Related Readings
Matthew 17:20; 19:14-15; 21:5; 1 Corinthians 1:26-29; 1 Peter 2:2

6

Naive Expectations

⎯⎯⎯∞⎯⎯⎯

He says to himself, "Nothing will ever shake me."
He swears, "No one will ever do me harm."

PSALM 10:6

THere's no such thing as a trouble-free life. To think otherwise is naive, presumptuous, and proud. Pride does this. It instills false confidence and unrealistic expectations. A man thinks himself immutable and omnipotent to conclude he'll always be free from adversity. Jesus said just the opposite. He taught that we're not of this world, therefore the world will hate us. This is not an invitation to a life of ease, but a guarantee of conflict. The naive pronounce an out-of-control optimism not based in reality. There's no way to totally shield ourselves from pain.

An opulent home or outrageous bank account can never keep us from suffering. Wealth sets us up for disappointment. Boasts are not buttresses, and self-confidence is a sorry security. Our confidence is in Christ, not in our ever-changing life of uncertainty. He is immovable and immutable. We vacillate. We change. We struggle, doubt, and fear. When life happens and the bottom falls out, we have a solid foundation in our Savior. He sustains us!

⎯⎯⎯∞⎯⎯⎯

"Pride goes before destruction,
a haughty spirit before a fall" (Proverbs 16:18).

Pride, on the other hand, brews naive expectations. This is the ruin of fools. When they succeed, their confidence bloats out of control. There needs to be a dose of humility that brings them back into the realities of everyday life. Engagement in the lives of others leads us to a more fulfilling life. Our success sets us up to serve others. To give back is to govern like God. This is what He expects. Godly expectations lead us down the road of service and selflessness.

So instead of insulating our lives from danger and risk, we follow the lead of the Holy Spirit. We ask, what does God think? Will this opportunity contribute to my spiritual growth? How does my spouse weigh in? What's best for my family? What will give me the most leverage for the Lord? We seek to align our expectations with eternity. It's a continual process of dying to ourselves and coming alive for the Lord. We should not expect a life of ease, but a life of obedience.

"In fact, everyone who wants to live a godly life in Christ Jesus will be persecuted, while evildoers and impostors will go from bad to worse, deceiving and being deceived" (2 Timothy 3:12-13).

How can I align my expectations with God's? What does persecution look like for the godly?

Related Readings
Isaiah 47:7; Daniel 4:34-37; John 15:19; Revelation 18:7

7

Stand Steadfast

In the LORD I take refuge.
How then can you say to me:
"Flee like a bird to your mountain."

PSALM 11:1

There's a time to stand steadfast and a time to flee. Make sure your motive for either is based on trust. Don't allow others to persuade you to run and hide when you need to stand and fight. Having faith in God may mean engaging in some uncomfortable activities. Don't run off just because you're afraid of being roughed up. Anybody can leave, but faith in God implores you to stay. Stand steadfast with your Savior. Trust Jesus when tempted to flee.

One of Satan's schemes is distrust. If he can get us to lose faith in our heavenly Father, he can influence our decision making with foolish thoughts. Satan is patient. He knows a little incremental doubt can lead to a large amount of distrust. Bad advice can be deceptive on the surface. This moment of decision is an opportunity for your faith to intersect with God's faithfulness. If you run, you'll miss refuge in Christ. Therefore stand steadfast.

Like the religious leaders who made fun of Jesus, some may say, "He trusts in God. Let God rescue him now" (Matthew 27:43).

Stability comes from standing steadfast with our Savior. Distrust, however, is like a frightened bird. It flutters here and there with no aim other than reacting to every distraction. There's nothing significant about a sparrow running scared. Anybody can run and hide in the face of difficult people or challenging circumstances. Does our life reflect total trust, or is our faith one of convenience? Strong faith stands steadfast.

Use this time of turmoil to trust the Lord even more. His calling hasn't changed. Stand steadfast. Stand steadfast in Him, and you'll stand steadfast in your marriage. Stand steadfast in Him, and you'll stand steadfast in your vocation. Stand steadfast in Him, and you'll stand steadfast in your purity. Stand steadfast in Him, and you'll stand steadfast in your friendships. Stand steadfast in Him, and you'll stand steadfast in your church. It's easy to leave when everyone else is fleeing. Nevertheless, we're convicted to stand steadfast and trust Him.

"Therefore, my dear brothers and sisters, stand firm.
Let nothing move you. Always give yourselves fully
to the work of the Lord, because you know that your
labor in the Lord is not in vain" (1 Corinthians 15:58).

Why does truth give me spiritual stamina? What truth do I need to believe and apply?

Related Readings
Psalms 51:10; 112:7; Proverbs 4:26; Philippians 4:1; 1 Peter 5:10

8

Flawless Words

———⋙———

And the words of the LORD are flawless,
like silver purified in a crucible,
like gold refined seven times.

PSALM 12:6

The words of the Lord are flawless. There's no dross in Christ's conversation. Men lie, but He is truth. Men deceive, but Jesus enlightens. Men flatter, but the Lord edifies. Men selfishly boast, but Jesus gives the glory to God.

Words can be wonderful or terrible, depending on their source. The Lord's words are rooted in righteousness. You can trust what God says. His words are appropriate and applicable. It's the words of heaven that make earth better.

The words of the Lord have stood the test of time. They've been tried by fire and have come forth faithful. The Holy Scriptures have received considerable criticism; some "scholars" have stripped them of miracles. Jesus warned there are severe consequences for adding to His Word (Revelation 22:18); God's Word does not need help. His words have survived the ravishing of faithless liberalism and loveless legalism. The Bible has been burned, belittled, and ignored. Nonetheless the Holy Scriptures are translated into more languages today than ever in the history of mankind. They've stood the test of time.

——— ⋙ ———

"Heaven and earth will pass away, but [Christ's]
words will never pass away" (Luke 21:33).

So take the Lord's flawless words by faith. Read them daily and apply them moment by moment. Study them and struggle with them. Seek to understand the context of the Bible and why God chose to speak specific infallible words through fallible followers. The Holy Spirit is the author of the Holy Scriptures (2 Peter 1:21). The pen of men moved under the instruction of divine inspiration. We have a stewardship of truth. Scripture is our handbook for holiness and happiness.

We honor and value His words when we take them to heart. We listen for instruction in our obedience. We listen for encouragement. We listen for rebuke. We listen to the Lord's flawless words because we know we're loved by Him. We have infinite access to wisdom. Like a precious jewel, the clarity and form of Christ's words are flawless and invaluable. They're matchless compared to man's meager trinkets. By God's grace we apply His flawless words to our flawed lives.

———∞———

"Your word is a lamp for my feet,
a light on my path" (Psalm 119:105).

How does God's Word light my path through life? What evidence is there that the Lord's words are flawless?

Related Readings
2 Samuel 22:31; Psalms 12:6; 18:30; Proverbs 30:5; Hebrews 4:12

9

Grateful for Good

I will sing the Lord's praise,
for he has been good to me.

PSALM 13:6

God has been good to us. His goodness is liberal and long lasting. His goodness is far reaching. Because He is God, He is good. Nothing soils the character of our Savior. The salvation we have in Jesus is good. The comfort we have in Christ is good. His wisdom is good. His answers to prayer, His forgiveness, and His grace are good. Heaven is good. We sing to the Lord because His goodness compels us. God's goodness accounts for all goodness we experience.

Gratitude gushes forth from a heart that has been tamed by the goodness of God. God has been good to us. The recognition of His goodness governs our gratitude. To the extent we remember how good God is to us, we'll appreciate our everyday life. Maybe He has given us a good job, good health, good sense, a good house, and a good family. It's the grace of God that allows us to experience His goodness. When we linger under the cross of Christ, we encounter the shade of His goodness. God is so good to us!

"Let the message of Christ dwell among you richly as you teach and admonish one another with all wisdom through psalms, hymns, and songs from the Spirit, singing to God with gratitude in your hearts" (Colossians 3:16).

When we're under the bright light of God's goodness, any bad influence is blinded. Gratitude and a bad attitude cannot coexist. Take the time to list what good things the Lord has done for you. Keep your list close by so when you're tempted to complain over trivial issues—traffic, someone's tardiness, waiting in line, not getting what you want—you can apply gratitude. Passion may possess an unbridled body, but patience controls a grateful soul. The Lord's goodness calls us to be good.

Goodness gives off goodness, rubbing off on others. God's goodness infects us so we can infect others with our good deeds. We're good to others because God has been good to us. Our goodness does not discriminate—we're good to others even when they're undeserving. Be patient with the one who doesn't deserve patience. Love the one who doesn't deserve love. Forgive the one who doesn't deserve forgiveness. Be grateful for God's goodness!

"The LORD is good to all;
he has compassion on all he has made" (Psalm 145:9).

How has the Lord blessed me? What does it mean to praise God for His goodness?

Related Readings
Psalm 73:28; Micah 6:8; Mark 10:18; Philippians 2:13; 1 Timothy 4:4

10

God Is Present

There they are, overwhelmed with dread,
for God is present in the company of the righteous.

PSALM 14:5

God is present in your predicament. You don't have to pray, "God be with us"; He's there already. He's there because He cares. He's there because you are extremely valuable to Him. God cherishes His children. He loves to give His own good gifts (Matthew 7:11). His presence alone is a present. He's present to give wisdom. He's present to give you direction. He's present to give you courage. In His presence there is peace. He is ever present.

God's presence is there to calm and convict us. His peace is what propels us forward by faith. Don't give up on doing the right thing. Sinful compromise for short-term satisfaction never ends well. Why put your family at risk by running after forbidden fruit? God hasn't left you. He doesn't wink at wicked deeds. He's right by your side to see you through this sinful temptation. Indeed the fruit of His presence is the fear of God. He reminds us to remain pure.

"How then could I [Joseph] do such a wicked
thing and sin against God?" (Genesis 39:9).

His presence is made manifest in a company of Christ followers. In community, the body of Christ is in full expression. Sin pushes us to seclusion. It's an illusion to think we can isolate ourselves from

Almighty God. But in authentic community there's nowhere to hide. In the presence of committed Christ followers, we feed our faith. Don't fight temptation alone. Tell someone. Stay engaged with the righteous. This is the presence of God personified.

Stay in the presence of God-fearing followers. This time of engagement with others facilitates our alone time with our heavenly Father. Stay hard after your heavenly Father in solitude and prayer. His presence is inviting you into intimacy. Design your life around a daily retreat into His presence. Look into His face and feel His love. In His presence He provides just what we need in the moment. Therefore persevere in prayer without ceasing. Be present in His presence!

—⊗⊗⊗—

"God is our refuge and strength,
an ever-present help in trouble" (Psalm 46:1).

What does it mean for the Spirit to be ever-present? How does the Spirit strengthen my spirit?

Related Readings
Genesis 4:16; Numbers 20:9; Jeremiah 52:3; Matthew 28:20; Hebrews 9:24

11

Heart Probe

———— ❧ ————

Though you probe my heart,
though you examine me at night and test me,
you will find that I have planned no evil;
my mouth has not transgressed.

PSALM 17:3

God's Spirit is interested in probing our heart. He knows the heart is the source of our speech and conduct. If our heart goes unexamined, we drift into a sick state of denial. We lose touch with reality and relegate others into our wrong thinking.

A healthy heart keeps us honest and engaged. It's the tender touch of Jesus that reminds us to look inward. Our heart can be a hindrance or a help to wise living. So how do we exercise the Spirit's probe?

A heart probe by God doesn't happen accidentally, but intentionally. Just as we daily determine to take care of the physical dimension of our heart, so also we're instructed to exercise our spiritual condition. We cannot spend all our time doing the work of God while ignoring the voice of God. Good works from an unguarded heart give only an illusion of selfless service. Our works cannot resolve a conflicted heart. Under the Holy Spirit's probe we see our true selves. In these moments of discovery we invite God's grace to strengthen our conflicted hearts.

———— ❧ ————

"It is good for our hearts to be strengthened
by grace" (Hebrews 13:9).

Our words, or the lack thereof, are evidence of what dwells in our heart. Sometimes the Holy Spirit checks our heart and moves us to silence. Trust transcends whatever trouble we face, and we exhibit long-suffering with the Lord and His people. This is a heart of faith. At other times the Spirit prompts us to speak up. We may be unclear of the outcome, but He gives us the courage to converse. This is a heart of boldness. Whether in silence or in speech, we submit to the Holy Spirit to govern our heart.

Your heart probe can come in a variety of ways. It may be a prescription of perpetual prayer that penetrates your heart with grace and forgiveness. It may be the treadmill of trust that builds endurance and creates within you a stronger heart of faith. Sometimes our Savior's stethoscope of conviction discovers sin that needs confession and repentance. A Spirit-probed heart produces right speech, spoken the right way. Intimacy with the Almighty hinges on a healthy heart.

"I the LORD search the heart
and examine the mind,
to reward each person according to their conduct,
according to what their deeds
deserve" (Jeremiah 17:10).

What heart motives is the Spirit probing in me? How can I be strengthened by God's grace?

Related Readings

2 Chronicles 6:30; Proverbs 22:11; Jeremiah 20:12; Revelation 2:23

12

Trust Perseveres

⸺ ❧ ⸺

For the king trusts in the Lord;
through the unfailing love of the Most High
he will not be shaken.

PSALM 21:7

Trust in God perseveres. It perseveres the higher it goes in responsibilities or the lower it goes in lost opportunities. Whether in the excitement of promotion or the discouragement of demotion, it still trusts God. In fact the more responsibility we gain, the more we need God. The more capable it seems we are, the more we realize we're incapable without Christ. Power tempts us to trust ourselves, but more power means more trust in God. Faith in the Lord's love perseveres.

Trust perseveres because it's buoyant in its belief in the unfailing love of God. The love of God stands secure in the face of suffering. The love of God licks the wounds of a lacerated soul. The love of God provides grace to forgive and forget. It continues in the face of ugly odds because the love of God knows what we can hope for in Christ. God's love draws us into intimacy with Himself. The Lord is trustworthy!

⸺ ❧ ⸺

"'Though the mountains be shaken
and the hills be removed,
yet my unfailing love for you will not be shaken
nor my covenant of peace be removed,'
says the Lord, who has compassion
on you" (Isaiah 54:10).

29

No one is higher than Almighty God. He is the Most High. We have the privilege, the opportunity, and the obligation to go right to the top. The Holy Spirit is God's gatekeeper. And by faith we can trust Him to intercede on our behalf. Our faith may be faltering in our confusion, but Christ clarifies. Don't give up because of the complexities of your current situation. Seek the Most High. He is wisdom. Trust perseveres.

The fruit of trust is perseverance. The lethal winds of adversity may attempt to uproot your faith but you persevere. Persevere in your marriage though culture gives you a pass for divorce. You persevere in your job even if you were passed over for someone less qualified. You persevere as a parent because this may be your time to mature. Allow Him to grow your character—to love you through this time of transition. Trust perseveres by God's unfailing love!

—◦◦◦—

"Let the morning bring me word of your unfailing love,
for I have put my trust in you.
Show me the way I should go,
for to you I entrust my life" (Psalm 143:8).

How can the Lord's unfailing love lead me through turbulent times? What is the fruit of perseverance?

Related Readings
Psalms 6:4; 13:5; Proverbs 20:6; Lamentations 3:32; Hosea 10:12; James 1:12

Trust Required

———— ⚬⚬⚬ ————

*Yet you brought me out of the womb,
you made me trust in you, even at my mother's breast.*

PSALM 22:9

God requires us to trust from our birth. In the beginning we're totally dependent on others. God uses doctors, nurses, and midwives to navigate us out of the birth canal. There's nothing we could do to gain access into this life other than wait on the warm embrace of others.

God Himself worked to bring us into the world. He conceived us and brought us out of our mother's womb. God stamped on our infant soul, "Trust in Me is required."

We were born desperately needy. The milk from our mother's breast sustained our life. She was our lifeline. She was the nurturer we trusted without reservation. In the same way, we depend on the milk of God's Word. We're babies in need of the elementary principles of the faith. At the genesis of our faith we were infants who drew life from our Savior Jesus. We trusted Him totally as our redeemer and refuge. Trust was required then and is still required now.

———— ⚬⚬⚬ ————

"Anyone who lives on milk, being still an
infant, is not acquainted with the teaching
about righteousness" (Hebrews 5:13).

In this life we never graduate from our Savior's school of trust. We're there until we graduate to heaven. It's a required course for Christ followers. He loved us in our infancy, and He doesn't cast us off in our riper years. He was our God when we left our mother, and He'll be our God when we return to mother earth. Be glad that God requires trust in Him. Trust connects us to Christ. The closer our walk with Jesus, the higher our level of faith.

In all relationships, trust is required. Don't replace trust in others with skepticism because of the few who've fractured your faith in people. If you trust God, you can trust others. Little faith in God leads to little faith in people. A big faith in God thinks the best of others. Don't be defensive with your spouse or co-workers. Trust them until they cannot be trusted. Trust facilitates trust. A robust and growing relationship with Jesus and people requires trust.

———∽∾∽———

"May the God of hope fill you with all joy and peace as
you trust in him, so that you may overflow with hope
by the power of the Holy Spirit" (Romans 15:13).

What's the result of total trust in God's trustworthiness? How can I grow in righteousness?

Related Readings
Psalms 37:5; 118:9; Proverbs 3:5-6; Isaiah 8:17; John 14:1; Acts 14:23

14

Trust Overcomes Fear

⬖

*Even though I walk
through the darkest valley,
I will fear no evil,
for you are with me;
your rod and your staff,
they comfort me.*

PSALM 23:4

Fear engages an ongoing assault on our heart and mind. If left unchecked fear can whip our imagination into a frenzy of anxiety. Though only an ounce of whatever we fear may come to pass, we tend to give it a ton of attention. It's madness when we're overcome by fear. It may be fear of death that dilutes our faith. It may be fear of failure that drives us to control. It may be fear of losing a job that becomes a self-fulfilling prophecy.

We're not alone in our fears. Jesus walks with us through our valleys. He may not deliver us out of the valley, but He most assuredly never abandons us there. He walks with us through the valley of doubt. He walks with us through the valley of shame. He walks with us through the valley of transition. He walks with us through the valley of disease. He walks with us through the valley of the shadow of death. A shadow assumes a light, so Christ is there to guide us. Trust overcomes fear.

⬖

"Blessed is the one
who trusts in the LORD,
who does not look to the proud" (Psalm 40:4).

Pain can create insecurity and confusion. But no amount of pain can separate us from the love of God. Pain may smother our soul, but we don't give up on God. We immerse ourselves in the psalms where David sometimes drowns in doubt, but by faith wisely lifts his soul to the Lord.

No one suffers well alone. Through the prayers of others, it's by the Almighty's help that we make it through.

Go to Christ for comfort. He draws us close with His rod and His staff. He heals our crushed heart with His caring touch. When we stray like lost sheep, He doesn't give up on us; rather, He goes after us.

Love isn't passive. It initiates contact, comfort, and connection. Love helps us make sense out of a senseless situation. The Holy Spirit brings clarity to our confusion, so we saturate our soul with truth, which flushes out our fears. Trust in the Lord overcomes fear!

⸺ ∞ ⸺

"'Where is your faith?' he asked his disciples. In fear and amazement they asked one another, 'Who is this? He commands even the winds and the water, and they obey him'" (Luke 8:25).

What fear do I need to replace with trust in the Lord? How do faith and obedience relate?

Related Readings
Isaiah 51:3; John 12:42; 20:19-21; 2 Corinthians 1:3; Hebrews 2:14-15

15

Qualifications for Closeness

───────── ∝∞ ─────────

Who may ascend the mountain of the Lord?
Who may stand in his holy place?
The one who has clean hands and a pure heart,
who does not trust in an idol
or swear by a false god.
They will receive blessing from the Lord
and vindication from God their Savior.

PSALM 24:3-5

Sincere worshippers of God long to be close to Christ. This is our eternal end game. This is the outcome we crave. Closeness to Christ places us in proximity for Him to wipe away our tears. Closeness to Christ reveals our sin and leads us to repentance. Closeness to Christ instills the best perspective, calming our heart and engaging our mind. The holy hill of the Lord is ascended by steps of repentance. Purity brings us closer to Jesus.

Closeness comes from cleanliness. We came from the dirt. We started out unclean. Dirt in our heart throws dust in our eyes. We struggle to see God when we haven't cleansed our heart. The pure in heart see God. But the impure of heart are like blind bats fluttering around in futility. We are from the dirt in the valley, while He is high atop His holy mountain. The snowcapped mountain of God is pure and clean. We ask the Holy Spirit to clean us up so we can make the ascent.

───────── ∝∞ ─────────

"Blessed are the pure in heart,
for they will see God" (Matthew 5:8).

35

So we approach the holy hill of the Lord with clean hands and pure heart. We pursue both an outward and inward purification. Both our behavior and our beliefs need sanitizing. Closeness to Christ comes when we align both actions and attitude. We wouldn't expect a server to bring our meal with soiled hands. Nor are we to serve our Lord with the dirt of denial under our fingernails.

God trusts those whom He holds close. He trusts them because they're nearby to hear His instruction and obey His command. They're hungry for His heart and thirsty for His trust. Closeness continually communes. It's not like the adult child who comes home only when something's needed. There's intentionality in intimacy. God blesses those who are close by. Stay cleansed and close to Christ!

━━━∞━━━

"The goal of this command is love, which comes
from a pure heart and a good conscience
and a sincere faith" (1 Timothy 1:5).

How is the Spirit purging my heart and moving me toward purity? What does it mean to have a good conscience?

Related Readings
Psalm 51:10; Proverbs 22:11; 2 Timothy 2:22; Hebrews 10:22

16

Shameless Hope

No one who hopes in you
will ever be put to shame,
but shame will come on those
who are treacherous without excuse.

PSALM 25:3

We're shameless when our hope is in our Savior Jesus Christ. Others may make fun of our simple faith, but they cannot shame us. Ironically, critics of faith are the ones to be ashamed. They're without hope. Misplaced hope is a sham. It leads to deep disappointment and disillusionment. Shame is the reward of sin. On the other hand, freedom is the fruit of hope. We have nothing to be embarrassed about when we hope in Jesus. Our Savior is never put to shame.

Hope, however, is often related to our hurt. In our pain, hope in Christ seems the most compelling. Our pain in suffering produces a need and capacity for hope. Suffering enlarges the heart by creating the power to sympathize. When we've been poor, we have more empathy for the poor. When we've combated disease, our prayers gravitate to the ill. It's out of our hope that we extend hope to the hopeless. Hopeful hearts look for those seeking the Lord.

"Guide me in your truth and teach me,
for you are God my Savior,
and my hope is in you all day long" (Psalm 25:5).

Our hope is reserved for us in heaven. Our heavenly Father owns our hope. In Him we never have to fear embarrassment. Our Savior's hope will never bring shame to our situation. No rational thinking person would say, "What a shame that Christians have forgiveness of their sins, abundant living on earth, and the hope of heaven." If anything, people without hope may be jealous and ashamed of their hopeless condition. Hope gives hope.

So heaven's hope is alive and well. It awaits the engagement of faithful followers of Jesus. Like a secret garden accessible by faith alone, we have the luscious environment of hope for our enjoyment. We can sit and smell the flowers of God's faithfulness. We can bite into the delicious, juicy fruit of God's peace. We can stand without fear in the warm light of the Lord's love. Hope may be lost for a season; when it is, don't be ashamed to continually seek the Lord. Seek the Lord while He can be found. You'll find hope in God. Hope is not ashamed of faith in Jesus!

"Seek the LORD while he may be found;
call on him while he is near" (Isaiah 55:6).

How can I grow my hope in the Lord? What does it mean to be guided by God's truth?

Related Readings
Psalm 62:5; Micah 7:7; Acts 24:15-16; Romans 15:13;
1 Timothy 6:17

17

Love and Truth

*For I have always been mindful of your unfailing love
and have lived in reliance on your faithfulness.*

PSALM 26:3

Walk in faithfulness to the truth, and be led by love. These are twins of wise living. Love is our leader and truth is our motivator. Love is our strategy, truth is our tactic. Love is our goal, truth is our inspiration. Love is our encouragement, truth is our obedience. We need both to become better followers of Jesus. Love and truth work together to bring us into balance.

This is why we look forward to the love of God as a guide for our faith. Faith trusts God to accomplish His own decrees. This is why we don't have to steal; we know God will provide for His children. This is why we don't have to seek revenge; God can and will handle oppressors in His own timing and way.

This is why we look ahead to the love of God. We follow the Lord and His love by faith—we trust and walk in His truth.

"Love does not delight in evil but rejoices
with the truth" (1 Corinthians 13:6).

We walk grounded in truth. Truth governs our faith and keeps us rooted in reality. Obedience to God's truth proves our love for Him. Truth takes us back to basics: "Who does Jesus want me to be?" We walk in truth because it preserves us from sinful behavior. Assurance of

God's promises will cause us to believe and behave like Christ. Like a GPS, truth guides us on the best path. Truth obeyed is best not delayed.

Stay away from those who stray from the truth. A companion of fools suffers harm (Proverbs 13:20). The fool who handles truth loosely may even be a pastor, teacher, friend, or business client. He'll lie even when the truth will do.

These are vain people. Don't sit with them and be drawn in by their sly charisma.

By contrast, those who walk in the truth may tell you things you don't want to hear. So listen when they prescribe doses of truth. The medicine may be distasteful, but once applied it will heal your heart. Walk in truth; walk with others who walk in truth. Follow love's lead as you walk with truth—Jesus is love and truth!

"God is love" (1 John 4:8); "Jesus answered,
'I am...the truth'" (John 14:6).

How can I walk and delight in the truth? What evil do I need to avoid?

Related Readings
Psalm 40:11; Zechariah 8:19; Ephesians 4:15; Colossians 1:5;
1 Peter 1:22

Confident in Crisis

———— ⊚∞⊙ ————

Though an army besiege me,
my heart will not fear;
though war break out against me,
even then I will be confident.

PSALM 27:3

A crisis can be seen as either an obstacle or an opportunity. Fear can creep into our feelings and begin to weaken our faith. An encamped enemy can instill as much dread as the actual battle. It's during interim times that we may fear the most. A crisis has a beginning and an end, but the consequences can continue. In crisis mode we learn to reject our instinct toward panic and desperation. Instead we trump feelings with faith. God has brought us safe thus far—He is faithful.

Fear erodes our confidence in Christ and replaces it with anger and defensiveness. We capitulate to our feelings from a desire to be in control. We think we have to take charge and operate from our own strength and ingenuity. However, "If God is for us, who can be against us?" (Romans 8:31). In the day of trouble He'll keep us safe in His presence. In crisis, we'll have joyful confidence in Christ.

———— ⊚∞⊙ ————

"In the day of trouble
he will keep me safe in his dwelling;
he will hide me in the shelter of his sacred tent
and set me high upon a rock" (Psalm 27:5).

Confidence in crisis means we're collaborative, not combative.

Confidence takes the high road of respect. There's no need to blame others or to beat them down with verbal attacks. Persuasive people are prone to pride. They're forceful with their feelings. Christ-confident people are patient. They seek the opinion of others. There's an invitation for intellectual engagement.

Our past experience may not be what's best for future direction. A confident and courageous leader can give up control and trust the Lord and others with the process.

Those who collaborate with Christ are positioned to be more than conquerors through Christ. Where there's no confidence in Christ, there's no continuance with Christ. Overcome your fears by faith in Jesus. He's just what you need. Hold your family, job, and opinions with an open hand. Trust Him and others in the process of crisis management. We can be confident in Christ in crisis. No fear by faith!

"He who began a good work in you will
carry it on to completion until the day
of Christ Jesus" (Philippians 1:6).

How can I grow my confidence in Christ as I face a crisis of faith? What does it mean to have joy in Jesus?

Related Readings
Job 6:20-21; Psalm 27:13-14; Luke 18:9; 2 Corinthians 5:6-9; 1 John 2:28

Voice of God

The voice of the LORD is over the waters;
the God of glory thunders,
the LORD thunders over the mighty waters.

PSALM 29:3

God's voice hasn't vanished. He hasn't lost His voice because of overuse. His vocal cords are strong, not strained. God doesn't cough or become congested. His voice is clear and intelligible. His voice is all around us; listen and be in awe. Thunder and lightning display His glory in the heavens. We hear His thunder and gaze up in fear and amazement. His voice reminds us of His glory. It's the Lord's majestic presence that thunders from above.

The glory of God governs the heavens. He's the source of light, heat, cold, and darkness. God is the creator and sustainer of earth. His creation continues because He continues to create. Just as humans are an ongoing creation of the Lord's, so earth is the Lord's ongoing creation. He resides in eternity but still engages with earth. His glory has not been gutted but rather validated by scientific explanation. Christ can be seen in all corners of His creation. His voice is clear.

"God's voice thunders in marvelous ways;
he does great things beyond our
understanding" (Job 37:5).

The power of His voice is applied in our life. His voice can be stern in discipline or tender in grace. The powerful voice of Jesus called Lazarus back from the dead, and on the cross He interceded to His heavenly Father for forgiveness on behalf of His enemies. Use your voice to pray for people who are dead in their sin and in need of a Savior. Lift up your voice on behalf of others who've offended or hurt you. God hears you; you're not a lone voice for the Lord.

God's voice is majestic and regal. He's enthroned above all His creation. Jesus is our King of kings and Lord of lords. When He speaks, we listen. His words matter most. The Bible is the wisdom of His words in written form. His voice speaks through the pages of Scripture. Take what He tells us there and obediently apply it to your life. Tell others what Christ tells you. Those of us who hear the voice of God cannot keep quiet. Be a clean conduit for His voice to speak!

―――∞∞∞―――

"Now, Lord…enable your servants to speak
your word with great boldness" (Acts 4:29).

What is the Spirit saying to my soul? How can I distinguish God's voice from competing voices?

Related Readings

Psalm 18:13; Jeremiah 6:10; Philippians 1:14; 1 Thessalonians 4:16

20

Secure, Not Shaken

———— ⬯ ————

When I felt secure, I said,
"I will never be shaken."
LORD, when you favored me,
you made my royal mountain stand firm;
but when you hid your face,
I was dismayed.

PSALM 30:6

Security rests in our Savior, not in our stuff. Stuff comes and goes—it's unreliable. But when Christ comes to dwell in our hearts, He remains. Because He is secure, we are secure. But we must beware lest we believe security resides anywhere other than the Lord. Our security isn't based on feelings, but faith. If our security depends on feeling secure—we'll be shaken by circumstances. But if our security rests on faith in Christ—no situation can shake us.

If our confidence is based on pleasant circumstances, our security is at risk. Our life becomes a rollercoaster of reactionary responses. If we feel good, we're secure; if we feel bad, we're insecure. If people like us, we're secure; if they don't, we're insecure. If we have money, we're secure; if not, we're insecure. If we're healthy, we're secure; if we're unhealthy, we're insecure. We eventually grow weary and wither under the whiplash of insecure living.

———— ⬯ ————

"Truly he is my rock and my salvation;
he is my fortress, I will never be shaken" (Psalm 62:2).

Don't place your security in success or failure. The fumes of success can smother your faith as fast as failure can extinguish your hope. The security we find in Jesus never changes. He is our rock and our refuge. He never moves. He's not shaken. Critics couldn't rattle Christ with their mockery and viciousness. His suffering only displayed more prominently His secure and pure behavior. Resurrection hope warmed His heart with calm assurance.

Left to our own efforts, we're anxious people. Whenever self seeks assurance outside of Christ, it becomes uncertain. The search for security results in insecurity when we marginalize our Master. Relationships come and go, but our relationship with Jesus remains intact forever. Doubt arises when we add anything to our faith in Christ. Therefore, develop your fidelity of faith. You're secure because your security rests on the eternal. Shun earth's securities and embrace heaven's. Faith in Jesus needs no outside help. By God's grace and love, the faithful are secure, not shaken!

"Though the mountains be shaken
and the hills be removed,
yet my unfailing love for you will not
be shaken" (Isaiah 54:10).

What does it mean to be secure in Christ? How can I keep success from shaking my faith?

Related Readings
Job 11:18; Psalm 112:7-8; Hebrews 6:19-20; 12:28; 2 Peter 3:17-18

Personal God

—✺—

But I trust in you, Lord;
I say, "You are my God."

PSALM 31:14

God is accessible and personal to those who call on His name by faith. He's not aloof, but engaging. God governs the universe while also taking time for those who come to Him. Trust in Him is a ticket to a personal relationship with Him. Trust is a bridge of belief that spans the canyon of a Christless life. It's when we trust Him that we're positioned to know Him. Relationship without trust is incapable of intimacy. When we know Him, we trust Him.

Adversity and challenges great or small compete with our trust in God. When it seems like our brand of Christianity isn't working, we're tempted to give up. We want to rebrand God to fit our selfishness. Since He's personal, we expect Him to bend toward our immature behavior. But we cannot give up on God. Christians will let us down, but not Jesus. Christ's care is personal and persevering. He's not going anywhere. We can laugh with the Lord as well as cry with Him.

—✺—

"The Lord has heard my cry for mercy;
the Lord accepts my prayer" (Psalm 6:9).

He is "my God" in the sense that He's my heavenly Father and I'm under His care and correction. In a similar way, others on earth serve as our mayor, governor, or president, and we're under their authority; we submit to the laws of the land for the sake of the whole. And because God is our ultimate authority, we submit to Him. Our rights are relegated to what God says is right. He is personal.

Avoid mistrust, and embrace trust in the Lord. Doubt leads to death and trust leads to life. God is personal and trustworthy. Our personal prayers are directly to Him. When you don't know what to pray, ask Him to align your heart with His so your desires become His desires. Intimacy with the Almighty leads to alignment with the Almighty. God gives us easy access so we can understand and apply His principles. He is personal for His purposes. So don't shun seeking your Savior. He can be trusted. He's your personal heavenly Father, for His glory!

"Where you go I will go, and where you stay
I will stay. Your people will be my people
and your God my God" (Ruth 1:16).

What does the Lord's personal care look like for my life? How can I grow deeper in relationship with Jesus?

Related Readings
2 Samuel 22:3; 1 Kings 5:4; Psalm 30:2; Matthew 27:46

Blessings of Forgiveness

*Blessed is the one
whose transgressions are forgiven,
whose sins are covered.*

PSALM 32:1

Forgiveness is full of blessings. The blessing of guilt's removal is a fruit of forgiveness. The peace of being in a right relationship with God and people is facilitated by forgiveness. The freedom to follow God's will, passionately and unashamedly, is fueled by daily forgiveness. Forgiveness frees the soul and enlightens the mind. It's a state of experiencing God's grace and mercy. Forgiveness takes away the stain of selfishness and dyes it with service. Sin is forgiven.

Foolish and naive are those who think they can continually keep God's law without the pardon of God's grace. Forgiveness is a daily requirement for those who want to keep short accounts with their Savior, family, and friends. Unless we repent of our sin from a contrite heart, there's no remission. Jesus gave His life so He could give us life. Jesus sweat blood so we could have sweet forgiveness. John, the forerunner of Jesus, taught repentance and forgiveness of sin.

"The word of God came to John…He went into all the country around the Jordan, preaching a baptism of repentance for the forgiveness of sins" (Luke 3:3).

The Bible describes a trinity of sin for the unforgiven. In our own strength our disobedience is labeled as transgression, sin, and iniquity. But the Trinity in heaven trumps the trilogy of sin. The Holy Spirit convicts us of sin and draws us into the love of our heavenly Father. His love leads us to Jesus, who gave His life on the cross to pay the penalty for our sin. We confess to Christ our need for His gracious forgiveness. In Christ we're free. Mercy comes to the man who repents.

Be a blessing by forgiving the unforgiven. We're forgiven by God so that we can forgive. Grace forgives those who don't deserve forgiveness. Unconditional forgiveness is freeing. Indeed, one reason you forgive others is for your own sake. Otherwise, unforgiving relationships cause a root of bitterness deep in your heart, robbing you of joy. Forgiveness prays for others to be healed, and in the process, *you* are healed. Forgiveness prayers prosper.

———∞∞∞———

"Whoever conceals their sins does not prosper,
but the one who confesses and renounces
them finds mercy" (Proverbs 28:13).

What sin do I need to confess and renounce? Who do I need to gladly forgive?

Related Readings
2 Samuel 12:13; Job 31:33; Psalm 31:2-5; Daniel 4:27; 1 John 1:9

Deliverance from Fear

———∞∞———

I sought the Lord, and he answered me;
he delivered me from all my fears.

PSALM 34:4

Prayer positions us to receive the peace of God. It's when we seek Him that we see Him. It's when we see Him that we're secure. As we travel across the choppy sea of life circumstances, we can become dizzy if we look down at the turbulent water. But if we keep our eyes fixed ahead on a stable object, we remain secure and feel safe. Jesus is our immovable object of belief. He replaces our furrowed brow of fear with a calm face of faith. The Lord hears our prayers.

No one has ever been sorry for seeking the Lord. It takes time and effort, but it's your best investment. Process your problems with prayer and you'll be the most productive. You cannot come to the best solutions in your own strength. The fruit that comes from replacing fear with faith is unlimited. We can rest assured as the Almighty leads us down a new path. He delights in determining a better way for you. Prayer opens the doors of God's plans and possibilities.

———∞∞———

"'For I know the plans I have for you,' declares the
Lord, 'plans to prosper you and not to harm you, plans
to give you hope and a future'" (Jeremiah 29:11).

This next season of your life is the Lord's reward for your faithfulness all these years. You've sought Him unashamedly and obediently.

Money was never your motive. Pride hasn't prodded you. Fame hasn't been your forte. You've sought Him with your unselfish service. You've sought Him with your humble obedience. You've sought Him by ministering to the needs of others. There's no safer, more secure place to be than in the process of seeking Him.

God expects to hear from you before you can expect to hear from Him. If you restrain prayer, He may refrain from grace and mercy. The more you think upon the Lord and the less you think of yourself, the better off you become. Seek Him and lose yourself, and you'll discover the best way. There's no need to fear the breaking off of a relationship. The Spirit is in the business of mending broken hearts. Seek Him, and He'll deliver you from your fears. Faith fossilizes fears!

"By faith he left Egypt, not fearing the king's anger; he persevered because he saw him who is invisible" (Hebrews 11:27).

What fear do I need to trust the Lord to deliver me through? Why is God's peace perfect?

Related Readings

Job 8:7; Psalm 40:5; Isaiah 55:12; Zechariah 8:15; John 12:42

24

Unanswered Prayer

───────── ∞ ─────────

When my prayers returned to me unanswered,
I went about mourning
as though for my friend or brother.
I bowed my head in grief
as though weeping for my mother.

PSALM 35:13-14

Sometimes God is silent, even when His children cry out for answers. The unfair becomes a test of faith that grows the prayer life of those who stay persistent with the Lord. No, He's not too busy answering the billion other prayers bombarding heaven, but He does want an unfeigned faith in His followers. God is not a cosmic Google waiting to give unlimited information to all requests. Too much data can break a spirit, puff up a mind, or confuse a heart.

Our heavenly Father knows what's best regarding unanswered prayers. We may not be ready to receive what we want or think we need. We seem stuck in a stage of suffering because we're learning the depths of dependence on God. We feel we're dog-paddling in a waiting phase because our patience needs to progress into perseverance. Our aloneness can suffocate us, but we breathe better spiritually in a close walk with Christ. Unanswered prayers produce prayer.

───────── ∞ ─────────

"Then Jesus told his disciples a parable
to show them that they should always
pray and not give up" (Luke 18:1).

Jesus says that even an unjust judge can be convinced of the right thing to do, but our heavenly Father doesn't have to be convinced of good actions. He is all good, and He knows what's best for His children. He wants us to be convinced of the next right thing.

A prolonged prayer process creates new convictions we cherish and cling to for comfort. For example, through prayer the Spirit may reveal anger in a pocket of your heart that He replaces with forgiveness. Unanswered prayer pushes us into unsearched places needing soul care. Humble prayers are always productive.

We remain in prayer to remain in Him. Our perspective grows in Christlike clairvoyance as we focus on our heavenly Father in His liberal love and holiness. When we grow familiar with the dynamics of faithful living, trust wins—suspicion never does. Prayer becomes like oxygen for our soul, lest we smother ourselves in worry. Like a needy widow we need assurance from Jesus, our righteous judge. Our Lord never sleeps; He listens intently and loves us passionately.

"Be joyful in hope, patient in affliction,
faithful in prayer" (Romans 12:12).

Why does God say no to some of my prayers? What's the purpose of unanswered prayers?

Related Readings
Isaiah 40:31; Luke 11:5-8; Romans 1:10; Ephesians 6:18; Colossians 4:2

25

Self-Flattery

There is no fear of God
before their eyes.
In their own eyes they flatter themselves
too much to detect or hate their sin.

PSALM 36:1-2

Self-flattery is foolish. It has no fear of God. Self-flattery follows a false faith that's forged out of convenience, not commitment. Self-flattery sees the self as the center of attention instead of Almighty God. It's enamored with itself. It defines and executes its own agenda. It's soft on sin. God-fearers, however, recognize their sin and flee from its presence. Respect for God flows from fear of God.

Self-flatterers hope that others share their high opinion of themselves. Self-flattery heaps praise on itself as a substitute for penance. To smooth over our conduct or soothe our own conscience sets us up for failure. We can justify anything, but we'd better be ready to suffer the consequences. There's a limit to our self-congratulation; eventually God and others grow impatient with our obnoxious ways. Our inability to own up to our actions lowers our standing with God and man. Self-flattery fails because it follows self instead of our Savior Jesus.

"You say, 'I am rich; I have acquired wealth
and do not need a thing.' But you do not
realize that you are wretched, pitiful, poor,
blind and naked" (Revelation 3:17).

There are many forms of self-flattery. When we think we're smarter than God but ignore the principles laid out in His Word, we flatter ourselves. When we think we have hope in heaven, but act like hell, we flatter ourselves. When we live for today, as if death is a million miles away, we flatter ourselves. When we treat others with contempt and expect them to follow us, we flatter ourselves. Self-flattery longs for approval but meets with only disapproval.

The road away from self-flattery is self-denial. Self-denial refrains from flattery. It's determined to know God. It's sensitive to sin and loves the Lord. The fear of God is in the forefront of those who deny themselves for the cause of Christ. Self-denial keeps God in holy awe and keeps self away from unholy worship. It makes much of God and little of self. Knowing God allows us to really know ourselves. Self-denial replaces self-flattery with faith in God. Faith in God frees us.

———∞———

"Do not think of yourself more highly than you ought, but rather think of yourself with sober judgment, in accordance with the faith God has distributed to each of you" (Romans 12:3).

What area of my faith is naive? How do I think more highly of myself than I should?

Related Readings
Proverbs 13:7; Hosea 12:8; 1 Corinthians 15:10; Ephesians 3:7

Enjoy Great Peace

*But the meek will inherit the land
and enjoy peace and prosperity.*

PSALM 37:11

Meekness is a bridge to blessing. It's an attitude God honors with the enjoyment of His great peace. Meekness meanders, moving in and out of the halls of heaven. A humble spirit is the manner by which our Master can move us forward in His will. Our meekness transports us toward absolute surrender and obedience to God. The meek trust God. It's the meek who want most to faithfully follow Jesus. Meek doesn't mean we're weak—we are strong in Christ.

Meekness is a conduit for what Christ has for us. He has an inheritance for His children. What is His is ours. He owns the land and everything upon it. We see His quiet white clouds cover the mountaintops like soft sheets. As the sun rises, its warmth pulls back the submissive cloud-sheets and introduces us to the day. His peace prods our pride to be still and know Him. He hushes our hurried spirit to be silent. The meek enjoy peace. Meekness is like Jesus.

"I am meek" (Matthew 11:29 KJV).

It's here, with meek Jesus, that we find rest for our souls.

Even as we suffer, we topple over tribulation with trust in Jesus while we rest in His great peace. Christ's consolation carries us along the way. His peace is a platform for His faithfulness to perform. Like an engaging drama on stage or in film, we watch and wait as the plot unfolds. If we jump to premature conclusions, we may get caught up in bad beliefs or false fears. So life is a stage where God's great drama plays out. His plot is still unfolding by faith. His will is being revealed. His cast of characters is still in development.

We may not have an abundance of stuff, but we have great peace. It's better to do stuff with our Savior than to have stuff without Him. He is our wisdom when we face complex circumstances. In crisis, we cling to Him. We silence our murmuring so we can be silent before Him. In silence before our Savior His great peace saturates our soul. It engulfs our edginess with eternal assurance. Fret not, but have faith in Jesus. Enjoy His great peace!

"All your children will be taught by the LORD,
and great will be their peace" (Isaiah 54:13).

How can I grow in meekness? What does it mean to inherit the land?

Related Readings

Psalm 119:165; Haggai 13:20; Matthew 5:5; Hebrews 13:20

27

Wait for God's Answer

⸻⸺∞∞⸺⸻

LORD, I wait for you;
you will answer, Lord my God.

PSALM 38:15

God's answer isn't always immediate. Our heavenly Father may not be forthcoming in His answer to prayer. We wait in our pain, and there seems to be no relief. We wait in confusion, and our circumstances grow more complicated. We wait for wisdom to harness our child's energy for God, and we find ourselves wanting. We wait in wonder over what we need to do at work. Answers from the Almighty may be absent for now, but the faithful wait.

We commit ourselves to Christ because we know He judges righteously. He can be trusted. He's not withholding His answer for His pleasure. In fact He may have already answered, and we've avoided hearing Him. Our activity can be an enemy to hearing God. We may need to slow down and stop trying to fix the faults of others. Seek the Lord and love Him. Seek His face and fear Him. God doesn't speak freely to those He can't trust, but to the trustworthy He gives insight.

⸺∞∞⸺

"Teach slaves…to show that they can be fully trusted,
so that in every way they will make the teaching
about God our Savior attractive" (Titus 2:10).

Our patience allows God to possess our soul. Hope in the Almighty's intervention and the power of prayer are what bring peace to a soul plagued by pain. In our adversity, the voice of the Almighty is near and clear. We just need to listen, really listen. Anger's roar may be filling the ears of our heart. Worry may mute our soul's capacity to listen to the Spirit. When we trust Jesus, we're in a position to hear Jesus.

Don't settle for anything less than the Almighty's answer. Look for the Lord's leading in His Word and among godly counsel. You'll find the richest solace in waiting for His wisdom. Why settle for the scraps of a quick solution when you can have the gold of God's solid strategy? Take your team or family through a process of discovering God's game plan. It takes time to trust, but the results bear the fruit of God's best. Rest in His refuge. He works while we wait!

———◈———

"The LORD is a God of justice.
Blessed are all who wait for him!" (Isaiah 30:18).

What does it look like to wait on the Lord? What blessings come to those who wait on God?

Related Readings

Isaiah 64:4; Hosea 12:6; Micah 7:7; Mark 15:43;
1 Corinthians 4:5

28

Life Is Short

————— ∞ —————

Show me, LORD, my life's end
and the number of my days;
let me know how fleeting my life is.
You have made my days a mere handbreadth.

PSALM 39:4-5

Sometimes we don't know what we know. We know God loves us, but we struggle with feeling loved by our heavenly Father. We know God can be trusted, but our faith becomes fragile under the fire of financial pressures. We know God is all-wise, but we forget and go to Him only as the last resort for instruction. We know we'll die soon, relative to eternity—yet we sometimes get sucked into a temporal trap. So we ask the Spirit to make real what we know.

Even heroes of the faith sometimes lost their focus on the brevity of life. David, who pursued God with passion, asked the Lord to let him know how fleeting his life looked. He needed to understand what he already knew. When we get caught up in the moment and wonder why Christ can't use us to His fullest, we forget how few our moments are in this life. So ask the Lord to remind you that there's no promise of tomorrow. Our life is the smallest of measurements. Only a handbreadth—a few inches.

————— ∞ —————

"You do not even know what will happen tomorrow.
What is your life? You are a mist that appears for
a little while and then vanishes" (James 4:14).

Life reminds us along the way of its temporal makeup. Funerals remind us that "death" escorts individuals into eternity. Each one of us, unless Jesus returns first, will be the center of attention at a black-attire event. What will those who knew you best say at your eulogy? Will the minister be able to say you carried on a love relationship with Christ? Will your spouse and children say you loved them unconditionally? Writing your obituary engages you with the end.

So the Lord expects us to live with the end in mind. Our investments in eternity are what matter most. People and God's Word are eternal. They're worthy of our investment of time and money. Our age is irrelevant when compared to the earth's age and the everlasting existence of our heavenly Father. Live for the Lord of the ages. The application of His purpose makes the most sense out of our short life. Life is short, eternity is forever. Live this life for Jesus Christ!

—∞∞∞—

"Teach us to number our days,
that we may gain a heart of wisdom" (Psalm 90:12).

How can I better live in the here and now? What does it mean to live like I'm dying?

Related Readings
Psalm 103:3; Lamentations 4:18; Daniel 5:26; Luke 12:18-20; Acts 18:21

29

Distrust the Proud

❊

*Blessed is the one
who trusts in the LORD,
who does not look to the proud,
to those who turn aside to false gods.*

PSALM 40:4

The proud are not trustworthy. They don't trust and they can't be trusted. They're self-contained in their own little controlling world. Their motives are suspect. It's all about their agenda and their priorities. There's a sense of urgency around what they deem important. Their only regard for others is to use them to accomplish their own end. Pride may give lip service to the Lord, but they trust in themselves. They even invoke the Lord's name, but mostly in vain.

So stay away from the influence of the proud lest you become like them. Keep your distance from those whose heart is hollow of humility. The proud may be attractive because of their accomplishments, but even the devil can get things done. Models worth following are those who are quick to give God the glory for their family and work success. They bow humbly before God's throne of grace and offer Him the fruits of their labor by faith. Trust the humble in heart.

❊

"All those who exalt themselves will be
humbled, and those who humble themselves
will be exalted" (Luke 18:14).

Be especially wary of those who portray an air of humility but mask a proud heart underneath. This may be the most hideous sin because it's unseen to the naive and naked eye. False humility wants you to believe what isn't true. False humility smiles when it isn't really happy. False humility serves, but only out of fear of the object of its service. False humility acts nice, but all the while resentment builds. False humility is pride in disguise. It's the worst kind of pride.

Deal daily with pride in your own heart and mind. Trusting God means not trusting in yourself. It's all about Him and His game plan. Success makes you think you're something. When you're tempted to that, run from taking credit for results. Humbly listen to the great thoughts of thinking people.

God's way is the best way. Tap into His truth. Trust Him with people and circumstances. Wait on the Lord; His way will prevail by prayer and patience. The humble hone in on heaven's agenda!

———∞———

"I leave within you
the meek and humble.
The remnant of Israel
will trust in the name of the LORD" (Zephaniah 3:12).

How can I walk humbly with Jesus? Who can I pray for who struggles with pride?

Related Readings
Deuteronomy 8:14; Job 40:11-12; Psalm 31:23; Ephesians 4:2; 1 Peter 5:6

30

Integrity's Stability

*Because of my integrity you uphold me
and set me in your presence forever.*

PSALM 41:12

Integrity is a stabilizing force in our life. It comes from God and is meant for God. Integrity is based on the strong moral principles of Jesus our Master. It's the foundation of what makes our faith compelling and attractive. Integrity marks the lives which are built on this strong slab of faith, with Christ as the chief cornerstone (Ephesians 2:20). It's your integrity that compels your children to come to you for counsel and advice. Integrity opens doors for your influence to flourish.

Maintaining integrity is not easy. Sometimes it costs us something. Maintaining your integrity may mean walking away from a relationship that reeks with inconsistency. Protect your integrity above all else. It's your credibility as a Christ follower. As you engage in financial dealings, stay away from gray areas. Gray areas can turn into a black hole of financial irresponsibility. They can drown you in the red ink of debt. Be honest about money.

"I know, my God, that you test the heart and are pleased with integrity" (1 Chronicles 29:17).

Sin seeks to sink our integrity. It wants to torpedo our testimony with temptation's allure. The Holy Spirit pricks our consciences early so we don't continue down a path of destruction. Our integrity places us in a strong and stable position to discern sin and stand against its assault. Since we're under our Savior's surveillance we can become an example of integrity.

Integrity matters because it positions us to be in the presence of God. This is the reward of walking in integrity. The Lord walks in lockstep with His honest and humble worshippers. His presence propels us to praise and obey Him. It's in His presence that we bring glory to God. Our awareness and acknowledgment of the Almighty ushers others into His presence. Our integrity allows us to invite others into experiencing God.

Steward your integrity well. It's God's instrument of righteousness reserved for His glory. Integrity stabilizes!

"David shepherded them with integrity
of heart" (Psalm 78:72).

How does God uphold me in my integrity? What area of my life needs to grow in integrity?

Related Readings
Job 2:3; Proverbs 11:3; Mark 12:14; Titus 2:7

31

Guiding Light

————— ⊗∞⊘ —————

Send me your light and your faithful care,
let them guide me;
let them bring me to your holy mountain,
to the place where you dwell.

PSALM 43:3

God is our guiding light. Without His light we're lost. At just the right time the beautiful beams of His light break through our clouds of uncertainty. He's the Master at making sure we can see the next step in His will. We can trust Him with this sequence of steps that mark His ways. He understands how contentment abides with Christ in the immediate, and hopes for His best in the future. Hold the Lord's lantern of truth and faithful care over your next step, and you'll see clearly.

There's a direct connection between truth and light. The more truth we learn and apply, the greater our capacity for illumination. Ignorance keeps us in the dark. Sin locks us in the fog of isolation. Where truth has been abandoned, there's little light to see the Lord's way.

As the sun sends forth its radiant rays, all nature gains life. By faith, follow His light.

————— ⊗∞⊘ —————

"You, Lord, are my lamp;
the Lord turns my darkness into light" (2 Samuel 22:29).

Sin may have suckered you into some dark place. You're afraid and unsure of what to do next. It may cost you an opportunity or a friendship, but it's time to leave the cold, clammy circumstance that withholds heaven's light. The reason you cannot see clearly may be due to the cloud of compromise hovering over your heart. Satan creates confusion. Christ gives clarity. Leave the dark days of your past behind you. Trust God with the unseen.

Lead others into the truth and light of the Lord. Take a risk and organize a Bible study over lunch at work. Take your team through a discovery process of timeless principles that make successful people and great companies. Don't be shy with your Savior. To pay for our sins, He hung naked for public display on the cross. So carry the torch of truth on His behalf. He has you in a place of influence at work and home to be a light of love. God is your guiding light!

"By day the Lord went ahead of them in a pillar of
cloud to guide them on their way and by night in
a pillar of fire to give them light" (Exodus 13:21).

What sin in my life is the Lord's light shining on? How can I be a light of hope to a friend?

Related Readings

Ezra 9:8; Psalm 4:6; Proverbs 20:27; Isaiah 60:1; Acts 13:47

32

Through God

Through you we push back our enemies;
through your name we trample our foes.

PSALM 44:5

Through God we get things done. What accomplishes great things is not our superior intellect, but God's wisdom and know-how. Everything depends not on our outstanding leadership, but on the leadership of the Holy Spirit, who gets us where we need to go. The biggest results are produced not by our financial prowess, but by the riches of the Lord's resources. Through God we best govern our lives.

Through God is how you get through fearful situations. Through God is how you get through death or divorce. Through God is how you get through teenagers. Through God is how you get through transitions. Through God is how you get through traumatic experiences. Through God is how you get through a financial quagmire. Through God is how you get through relational reconciliation. In your own strength, you slip back—in His strength, you overcome obstacles.

"'Not by might nor by power, but by my Spirit,'
says the LORD Almighty" (Zechariah 4:6).

In union and communion with Christ, He works wonders. There's nothing about God that isn't good and worth emulating. It's through the engrafting of His character into ours that we pay Him the greatest compliment. It's in and through the Lord's shaping of our soul that we become more sensitive to His Spirit. Only as we cooperate with Christ can we experience Him working through us. Don't underestimate how much God wants to work through you.

Therefore, do things through God; you won't regret the results. The Lord's results are lasting because they're aligned with His sovereign plan. No one can thwart what God can do. By your faith, He uses you to accomplish His will. A broken and submissive follower of Jesus with average ability is exceedingly superior to a self-reliant believer with greater skills and potential. Stay focused on what the Spirit can do through you, not on what you can do for Him. God gets you through.

———∞———

"That is why, for Christ's sake, I delight in weaknesses, in insults, in hardships, in persecutions, in difficulties. For when I am weak, then I am strong" (2 Corinthians 12:10).

What situation do I need to trust the Lord with to get me through? Who has God provided to help me get through?

Related Readings
Haggai 1:3; Zechariah 7:12; John 3:17; Acts 2:22; 21:19; Romans 1:4

33

Enthralled by Beauty

Let the king be enthralled by your beauty;
honor him, for he is your lord.

PSALM 45:11

Your beauty enthralls God. It is first the beauty of your belief in Christ that attracts you to Almighty God. When you embrace His Son as your salvation, you gain absolute approval and blessing from your heavenly Father. There's nothing more you can do to gain God's acceptance than to accept His Son Jesus. This makes you beautiful to Him. Your breathtaking beauty of faith in Him compels Christ to romance you. Unfeigned faith calls for God's love.

Your internal attractiveness makes your external appearance and attitude inviting. God starts by beautifying the heart before He brings the body into His submission. A body can be beautiful, but without a clean heart it isn't attractive to Christ. Beautiful people who love Jesus are called to point people beyond themselves to God. As outward beauty fades, inward beauty grows more attractive. Aged beauty in Christ is easy on the eyes of the soul. God makes attractive those who are His own.

"From Zion, perfect in beauty,
God shines forth" (Psalm 50:2).

Dads have the opportunity and responsibility to tell their daughters they're beautiful. As the Lord's representative, look them in the eye and express the blessing of their beauty. Tell them how you love their smile and the joy it brings to your heart. Describe to them the beauty of their pure eyes as a reflection of their clean heart. Use respectful words and courteous acts to affirm their sensitive hearts. Daughters desperately need their dad's approval.

Let the Lord love you in the beauty of His holiness. Just as the church is the bride of Christ, so we have entered into an individual and intimate relationship with Him. We are beautiful to God, and He is beautiful to us. There's a mutual attractiveness that mirrors marriage. See yourself as God sees you in Jesus: beautiful and accepted. See Him as He is: lofty and lovely. Worship Him in the beauty of His holiness. Beauty attracts beauty. Without Christ, we're beastly. In Christ, we're beautiful. Rest in and enjoy everlasting beauty!

"'Leave her alone,' said Jesus. 'Why are you bothering her? She has done a beautiful thing to me'" (Mark 14:6).

How has Jesus made the ugly areas of my life beautiful? How can I best honor Him?

Related Readings
Psalm 116:15; Proverbs 31:30; Isaiah 61:3; Mark 14:6; 2 Peter 1:3-8

34

God Reigns

God reigns over the nations;
God is seated on his holy throne.

PSALM 47:8

God reigns over the entire earth. The sun never sets on the omnipresent shadow of our Savior Jesus. He's the greatest in power, high and lofty in dominion, preeminent in wisdom, and elevated in excellence of glory. Our God reigns. He reigns in war and in peace. He reigns in crisis and in calm. He reigns in economic catastrophe and in economic prosperity. He reigns over good and evil. He reigns over nations and individuals. Our God reigns.

He reigns from His holy throne. His is not a throne soiled with corruption and self-serving. His throne is full of grace and truth. His throne is marked and defined by holiness. It has never been stained with sin, corrupted by cover-up, or defiled by injustice. God never sits dismayed or experiences a dilemma. He sits in serene security. His throne dispenses wisdom, grace, and mercy. We can approach His holy throne boldly.

"Let us then approach God's throne of grace with
confidence, so that we may receive mercy and find
grace to help us in our time of need" (Hebrews 4:16).

God reigns over the human heart. It's here that we can submit to or spurn the Almighty's authority. It's in submission to our reigning King

Jesus that we come to know His will for our lives. Obedience leads to opportunity. Because our God reigns, He can be trusted. His rules are for our good. Christ is not a cosmic killjoy. So love Him, and you'll love to follow Him. It's easy to follow an unconditional lover. Our God reigns in love and holiness.

We have every reason to celebrate Christ's reign. His kingship brings praise to our lips. Our Lord reigns. Hallelujah! We have no real reason to worry or stress out, because our God reigns. We can put the kibosh on our murmuring because our God reigns. We can sleep peacefully because our God reigns. We can let go of control and not be controlled because our God reigns. We can give Him our grief, sorrow, and sin because He reigns. Our God reigns now and forevermore. Amen and amen!

———∞∞———

"[Christ] has made us to be a kingdom and priests to serve his God and Father—to him be glory and power for ever and ever! Amen" (Revelation 1:6).

What does it look like for God to reign over my life? What do I need to leave at His throne of grace?

Related Readings
1 Samuel 12:13-14; Psalms 99:1-9; 146:10; Isaiah 52:7; Revelation 19:6

35

Master Meditation

—⚬⚬—

Within your temple, O God,
we meditate on your unfailing love.

PSALM 48:9

Wise men and women meditate on God. They know Him through His written Word, a personal letter from their heavenly Father full of His unfailing love. And the primary purpose for listening is the transformation of the hearer. It's not to gain more information so we can impress others with our knowledge. The Lord's desire is that we listen and become more like Jesus. As we contritely meditate, we declare Almighty God's mastery over our life.

If we're not careful, we cringe at what Christ may say, listening only to what we want to hear. Humble meditation means we listen to the full counsel of God, which is indiscriminate in its understanding of His character and plan. Meditation on our Master leads to massive soul transformation. It unleashes a work of grace in our hearts that gyrates to future generations. Meditation on God becomes the Spirit's system for governing our inner being.

—⚬⚬—

"May these words of my mouth
and this meditation of my heart
be pleasing in your sight,
LORD, my Rock and my Redeemer" (Psalm 19:14).

We can meditate both personally and corporately. We individually hear God speak. His intimacy is unrivaled in the way He loves us specifically for who we are. He has a personal plan and a purpose for us that we come to appreciate and understand in solitude and silence. But we also meditate on our Master among His people. This is our gathering for collective praise and thanks. Our spirit engages with His transcendence and holiness through worship with others.

Listen to the Lord through writing. Journal what Jesus is saying to you. Pen to paper pulls out what's within your heart. It exposes who you are and who He is, and how you can become more like Him. Consider calendaring two days of worship with Christ. The more you meditate on His unfailing love, the more you're loved by Him and the more capable you are of fulfilling His greatest command of loving Him and others. Meditation migrates you toward your Master Jesus. Authentic meditation moves you to be mastered by your Master!

<hr />

"May my meditation be pleasing to him,
as I rejoice in the LORD" (Psalm 104:34).

What makes my meditation pleasing to the Lord? How do I feel when I meditate on God's unfailing love for me?

Related Readings

Genesis 24:63; Joshua 1:8; Psalms 77:12; 119:97; Hebrews 10:7; 2 Timothy 4:13

36

Honor God

⟨⟨⟩⟩

Those who sacrifice thank offerings honor me,
and to the blameless I will show my salvation.

PSALM 50:23

Honoring God is our obligation as Jesus followers. It's not an option but an opportunity to afford praise and thanksgiving to the Almighty. The honor of God places the focus of our appreciation on the object of our affection: Jesus. Such honor is far beyond mere language from our lips—it's the habit of our delicious living. Our life is honorable when gratitude motivates our actions. It's a celebration of salvation in Christ. Gratitude honors God.

Our worship honors God when our behavior matches our beliefs. This is why we come before Christ in confession and repentance. It's an honoring of the standards He has set with His life and words. To receive Jesus's salvation and then ignore Him until we get to heaven is dishonoring to our Lord.

We go to God in praise because we need it—and because He deserves and expects it. He's honored in heaven and on earth by our sober acts of submission and praise to Christ.

⟨⟨⟩⟩

"Our citizenship is in heaven. And we
eagerly await a Savior from there, the
Lord Jesus Christ" (Philippians 3:20).

In our acts of honor, we hear the voice of the one we are honoring.

Honoring improves our hearing and brings clarity. When we honor God and people above ourselves, we gain perspective. Self-honoring drains the life from a situation, while offering honor gives life. We honor others when we serve them. We honor others when we're kind. We honor others when we involve them in our decision making. We honor others when we invite them to special occasions: showers, weddings, funerals, anniversaries. Honor involves others.

God honors those who honor Him. What an honor to be honored by God! He honors us with His love and intimacy. He honors us with responsibilities and success. He honors us with wisdom. He honors us with blessings undeserved. He honors us with friends and family. He honors us with health and healing. He honors us by calling us His own. Our honor invites His honor. By God's grace, do the honorable thing. Honor prepares His way for our life!

"Those who honor me I will honor, but those who despise me will be disdained" (1 Samuel 2:30).

How can I best honor the Lord with my life? In what ways does gratitude for my salvation honor God?

Related Readings
Psalm 103:20; Mark 7:6; Romans 12:9-10; 1 Corinthians 6:20

37

Broken by God

My sacrifice, O God, is a broken spirit;
a broken and a contrite heart
you, God, will not despise.

PSALM 51:17

Brokenness by God is beautiful to Him. It's His passageway to purity. It's His entrance into intimacy. It's His plan for our maturity in the faith. We need the tender touch of our Lord to lead us from a hardened heart to one broken before Him. An unbroken heart rivals God. A broken heart aligns with God. Unbroken, we're like a wild stallion. We need a "heart whisperer" from heaven to tame our spirit. We need God's bridle of brokenness to bring us under submission. If we buck the Holy Spirit's breaking—we're in for a rougher ride. He breaks us to build us up.

Some broken things are discarded. They're done away with because they're more easily replaced than repaired. We can't drink any longer from a broken glass. Our heart, on the other hand, is most useful after it's broken. A heart is never at its best until then. Brokenness brings out what's on the inside. It reveals where there's still a rascal in rebellion. It's in our brokenness that divine restoration takes place. A broken heart experiences God.

"I live in a high and holy place,
but also with the one who is contrite
and lowly in spirit" (Isaiah 57:15).

79

Brokenness is both an event and a process. Your salvation broke you of unbelief and brought you into right standing with your Savior. However, the Holy Spirit is still breaking your behavior by conforming you into the image of Christ. It's a process of your pride decreasing and your humility increasing. Don't be gullible, thinking you're over your need for a work of God's grace. Brokenness is a process of becoming more like Jesus. He tames you to trust Him.

Brokenness is God's way to blessing and change. He breaks our will and restores us to His will. He breaks our spirit and restores us to the security of His Spirit. He breaks our pride and restores us to His humility. He breaks our stubbornness and restores us to His sensitivity. He breaks our harshness and restores us to His kindness. He breaks our greed and restores us to His generosity. He breaks our lust and restores us to His love. He breaks our disobedience and restores us to His obedience. Brokenness is our transformation by God's grace and truth.

"I will give you a new heart and put a
new spirit in you" (Ezekiel 36:26).

What positive outcomes result from brokenness? What habit of mine needs to be broken by God?

Related Readings
Psalm 4:7-8; Ezekiel 11:19; 18:31-32; Romans 12:1-2;
1 Timothy 1:5

38

Trust Grows Love

*I trust in God's unfailing love
for ever and ever.*

PSALM 52:8

Trust in God is the soil in which our love grows. Like a robust olive tree full of branches bearing luscious fruit, trust encourages growth across the limbs of our life. Trust tears down our walls of fear. Trust allows us to outlast our critics. Trust brings to fruition a harvest of hope and patience. Trust keeps us from reacting unjustly. Trust causes good things to grow. Our faith grows. Our humility grows. Our love grows. Our holiness and grace grow. Our fear of God grows. Our character grows. It's trust in our Savior that grows us up.

There's no doubt that God's unfailing love can be trusted. No one has ever overdrawn the Almighty's account of love. You can depend on the love of God. He won't fail you when you need Him most. Others may walk away when you lose your way, but you cannot lose the love of God. You may feel deserted in your despair, but God's loving care is still there for you.

"Love never fails" (1 Corinthians 13:8).

Sometimes it's hard to see the forest of our heavenly Father's love for the trees of fear that stare us in the face. This is where we need to pause and trust. Trust that God still loves you even when you represent Him poorly. Trust that He still loves you even though those around you don't seem to care. Trust that He still loves you in the loss of your job.

Being loved by God is just the beginning. Christians are a conduit for Christ in His cycle of love. We're His love agents. Your trust in Jesus causes your love to grow to greater heights. His goal is for the fruit of His love to weigh down the branches of your belief. Your fruitful loving life becomes attractive and inviting to others. They want to draw near to the light of the Lord's love that shines through your soul. They want to be close to your character so they can pluck some of your lovely fruit and partake. God's love in your life is a beacon of hope. Love is a remedy for rebellion. When the prodigal son came home, his father first loved him. Trust in God's unfailing love grows our love!

———∞———

"In your unfailing love you will lead
the people you have redeemed" (Exodus 15:13).

Why is God's unfailing love so trustworthy? How does the Spirit want to grow my love of others?

Related Readings
Psalm 33:18-22; Isaiah 54:10; Hosea 10:12; Luke 15:20;
Colossians 1:4-6

39

Foolish Denial

⸻⸎⸻

The fool says in his heart,
"There is no God."
They are corrupt, and their ways are vile.

PSALM 53:1

Fools foolishly deny God. It's an excuse for loose living without the Lord. It's the rejection of righteousness. It's their hope that there is no God. Somehow godless belief justifies godless behavior. Denial of God is a pushback against His principles. To deny God is to deny His law. Denial of God's law leads to moral and ethical anarchy. There's no stability in a society where everyone does what's right in his or her own eyes (Judges 21:25). It's corruption in the eyes of Christ.

"Corrupt" is how God describes those who deny Him. They're corrupt and vile. These aren't just nice people who've lost their way. They shake their faithless fist in the face of God and demand that He disappear. This is what they did to Jesus. He came claiming to be the Christ. He was the Messiah for the salvation of mankind. But some men didn't want God. They were a "god" unto themselves. So they paid Jesus evil for good. They attempted to kill God. But Christ's crucifixion and resurrection drove the final nail into their corruption. God is not dead.

⸻⸎⸻

"I am the Living One; I was dead, and now look,
I am alive for ever and ever!" (Revelation 1:18).

As a follower of Jesus you may feel the pressure from outside forces to deny Him. Don't allow the persuasion of unprincipled people to force you into faithlessness. Atheism is for the uninformed. How can someone deny the existence of God when our understanding of all knowledge is relatively minimal? An atheist can only "say" in his heart, while Christians can "know" in theirs. We know because the evidence for God is overwhelming. We know because we've experienced God. We know because we know Him.

Be there for those who finally figure out that atheism isn't working for them. A crisis may turn them to Christ. A friend may reveal an authentic faith, and the seeker desires the same. Reading the Bible may bring them to their heavenly Father. Pray for the Holy Spirit to penetrate the deceived heart of an atheist. The reality of God shines through you. Spirit-filled Christians are a compelling case for Christianity. Yes, by grace—love atheists to the Lord!

"God our Savior…wants all people to be saved and to come to a knowledge of the truth" (1 Timothy 2:3-4).

Why is it foolish to deny God's existence? Who can I love well in spite of their unbelief?

Related Readings

Proverbs 14:16; Isaiah 32:6; Luke 12:20; 2 Corinthians 11:17; 2 Timothy 1:12

40

Perseverance Pattern

⸺⸺⸺ ⧜ ⸺⸺⸺

Surely God is my help,
the Lord is the one who sustains me.

PSALM 54:4

Our Savior sustains us by His strength. Christ carries us with His compassionate care. Our heavenly Father is forever loving us to Himself and sending us forth into life's fray by faith. The Lord looks to leverage our life for His longevity. His desire is that we not give in or give up. He's a God of determination. He expects His children to be the same. A thimble of Christ's aid is better than heaps of man's help. It's in prayer that you receive God's help to persevere. The Spirit gives peace and a quiet confidence. Christ is our divine champion.

We have no need to fret because our heavenly Father is here to help. Sometimes the pressures at work pour over us like the constant pelting of marble-sized hail. We're bruised, beat up, and unsure of ourselves. People's nitpicking makes us feel we're about to be nibbled to death. Nothing seems to be going right, so we start thinking we need to quit. But persevere—don't quit before God is done with you. His best is yet to come.

⸺⸺⸺ ⧜ ⸺⸺⸺

"We also glory in our sufferings, because we know
that suffering produces perseverance; perseverance,
character; and character, hope" (Romans 5:3-4).

God is our help in times of trouble. In Him we trust. When we see

Him, we persevere. It's easy for our eyes to remain riveted on problems. Immediate issues can overwhelm us if we give their influence full access to our attention. But the Lord would rather have us linger with Him. Replace unproductive time of worry with productive time in prayer. When you gaze on God, fears fade away. Little do we care for the defiance of our foes when we have God's defense.

God's grace will sustain you. His grace is sufficient for your specific situation. You can move forward by faith. Don't allow a financial setback to keep you from going to God. He owns everything. He has what you need to make it through a major transition. God is already on your side, so stay by His. You have His mammoth mercy and loving-kindness to draw on in your discouragement. Your Savior, not stuff, is your sustainer. Jesus is always with you!

------ ∞ ------

"You need to persevere so that when you
have done the will of God, you will receive
what he has promised" (Hebrews 10:36).

How is God's help superior to any other? What does Christ offer to sustain me in difficulty?

Related Readings
Psalms 3:5; 146:9; 147:6; Proverbs 18:14-15; Isaiah 50:4-5; Hebrews 11:27

41

A Friend's Rejection

*If an enemy were insulting me,
I could endure it…
But it is you, a man like myself,
my companion, my close friend.*

PSALM 55:12-14

The worst kind of rejection may be the rejection of a friend. You expect it from an enemy, but not a friend. It doesn't make sense that someone you communed with around Christ would come back and crush you with rejection. Rejection integrated with religious pretense is rough. It challenges our trust in people in general, and our faith in God in particular. You don't know whether to lash back or to languish in disillusionment. A friend's betrayal is frightening.

A reproach from intimate companions will cut to the heart. They know where we're vulnerable. They know how to exploit our struggles and take advantage of our goodwill. It's as if you've been emotionally naked with someone, and now feel exposed—unsafe. What happened to the person you once knew? How could you have been so deceived? It may have been a decade of deceit in your marriage vows. It may have been financial fraud over a long period of time. Or a hidden addiction that hijacked your trust and respect. Rejection hurts.

"Blessed are you when people hate you,
when they exclude you and insult you" (Luke 6:22).

Our Lord Jesus trusted someone to manage the disciples' money.

He was close to Christ in proximity but far away in faith. For Judas, it was all about the cash. It was money that motivated him in the beginning, and money that was his downfall in the end. Money-motivated men may be pleasant on the outside, but they're full of themselves on the inside. Be careful—get to know someone before you heavily invest. Perhaps in time they can be trusted.

Avoid the temptation to reject those who've rejected you. Under the influence of the Holy Spirit, our right response is to forgive their failings, regardless of how hurtful their behavior. Without God's grace and the accountability of a committed community of believers, we all become deceivers. Rejection by a trusted friend is fiendish and false-hearted. But we're called to be forgiving and kindhearted. Don't stoop to their standards. By God's grace, rise above rejection!

—◦◦◦—

"Brothers and sisters, if someone is caught
in a sin, you who live by the Spirit should
restore him gently. But watch yourself, or you
also may be tempted" (Galatians 6:1).

How does grace handle betrayal? How does Christ's acceptance help us when we're rejected by a friend?

Related Readings
Proverbs 2:1-6; John 12:48; Romans 14:1; 15:7;
1 Corinthians 16:11

42

Purpose Fulfillment

‐‐‐‐‐‐‐‐‐‐‐∞‐‐‐‐‐‐‐‐‐‐‐

I cry out to God Most High,
to God, who vindicates me.

PSALM 57:2

Our gracious God promises to give us wisdom in His ways. He wants us to experience His eternal aim for His glory. The fulfilling of His purpose started when we placed our faith in Jesus. This was our contract with Christ that placed the responsibility of fulfilling His purpose at the feet of our heavenly Father. Our Lord finishes what He begins. Whatsoever the Lord takes in hand, He will accomplish. So we trust the Almighty with the fulfillment of His purpose for our life.

Prayer prepares us to harvest heaven's purpose for us. We cry out to the Most High because nothing and no one is any higher. God is the divine decision maker. He is *our* Maker. To understand the purpose of our lives, we can go nowhere else but to the Lord Jesus Christ. We cry out to Christ because He has adopted us. Our heavenly Father defines our purpose; prayer positions us to be led by the Holy Spirit so that our purpose is fulfilled.

‐‐‐‐‐‐‐∞‐‐‐‐‐‐‐

"He who began a good work in you will
carry it on to completion until the day
of Christ Jesus" (Philippians 1:6).

Prayer to God is proof of our trust in God. When we send our prayers to heaven, God will send help down from heaven. Trust can become trivial if persistent prayer doesn't back it up. Prayer brings trust into the reality of God's promises for our life. Prayer is potent because it aligns us with the ways of Almighty God.

Yes, define your God-given purpose. Use this definition as a filter for decision making. This becomes your accountability to God and others and enables you to say no to other things.

Lean into the Lord to lead you in His plan for your life. Once you establish His purpose for you, leverage it for others. Use your strength of position to help others discover their God-given purpose. Have them list their gifts, skills, passions, and experiences. Pray with them about how God wants to collate their assets for Christ. No season of life is insignificant in the Lord's eyes. Don't wish away where you are today. By faith, you can be sure that Christ is currently fulfilling your purpose. Affirm that your goals are God-given, and trust Him with their fulfillment!

———⊂∞⊃———

"But when the set time had fully come,
God sent his Son" (Galatians 4:4).

What's the role of prayer for us in fulfilling God's plan? How can I adjust my goals to reflect God's?

Related Readings
1 Chronicles 28:12; Job 5:11-12; Psalms 20:4; 33:11;
2 Corinthians 1:15-18

43

Poisonous Pride

———— ❦ ————

Their venom is like the venom of a snake,
like that of a cobra that has stopped its ears.

PSALM 58:4

Pride is poisonous in its effect. Like a slithering snake, it sneaks up on its prey and delivers deadly venom with a startling and painful bite. Its venom travels quickly to all parts of the body with paralyzing impact. Without the salvation of a properly applied serum, the victim's life is sadly snuffed out. In a similar way pride looks to strike selfish prey. It can quietly coil in the bushes of a heart in crisis and cause it to lash out. Pride slithers through our selfish desires and ego. It strikes when we don't get our way. Pride is deadly.

It kills relationships and strikes fear in those in its path. Pride's insecurity lies in false faith. We cannot be authentically intimate with Jesus and remain secure in ourselves. True communion with Christ transfers our trust to Him. He transforms us into humble and obedient followers. The serum of humility eventually overtakes the poison of pride and makes us rest secure in Christ. Humble thinking softens our heart, subdues our stubbornness, and opens our ears to wise counsel.

———— ❦ ————

"Do not conform to the pattern of this
world, but be transformed by the renewing
of your mind" (Romans 12:2).

Sadly, a closed mind leads to a joyless heart. But the humble ask,

What's the wise thing to do? What's best for the enterprise, the team, the family?

Pride is hard to see in the mirror but easy to see in someone else. How can we truly hear from our heavenly Father if we don't hear from His children? Listening to the Lord requires listening to people. He speaks through the stakeholders in our lives. Our spouse, our parents, our children, and our peers, friends, and acquaintances can all be God's messengers of mercy. Humility listens with the intent to learn.

Come clean with Christ, with a contrite and teachable heart. There's no need to fear questions. Even if the questioner is prideful, resist the temptation to defend. Allow a thoughtful and respectful process to prove what's right. Humility listens intently, understands thoroughly, and responds appropriately. In prayer, we listen to the Lord. In conversation, we listen to people. Avoid the pain of pride before it strikes, but when it does—quickly inject the serum of humility!

"The prudent see danger and take refuge,
but the simple keep going and pay
the penalty" (Proverbs 27:12).

What prideful reactions cause me and others pain? How can I respond with a humble, teachable heart?

Related Readings
2 Chronicles 7:14; 32:25; Psalm 40:4; Proverbs 3:34;
1 Corinthians 5:1-5

44

Request for Restoration

⚬⚬⚬

You have rejected us, O God, and burst upon us;
you have been angry—now restore us!

PSALM 60:1

Restoration means we're in right relationship with God and others. Restoration with God is the right request, but it happens only when we're willing to come clean with Christ. We cannot simultaneously be restored by God and rebel against God. It doesn't work this way in the Lord's economy of relational wholeness. Restoration follows repentance. When the one running from God finally grows weary, they're ready for repentance. Obedience positions us for restoration.

Disobedience forms a breach in our beliefs. It causes cracks in an already fragile faith in Christ. Disobedience dismisses doctrine as too restraining. Disobedience declares itself superior to its Savior. It thinks its own plan is better than God's plan.

Sometimes we're our own worst enemy. Disobedience is disillusioned and foolish. It forgets to apply simple faith in Christ. When we fail to obey, we open ourselves up to a failure of faith. A fractured faith needs restoration by God.

⚬⚬⚬

"When you…return to the Lord your God and
obey him…then the Lord your God will restore
your fortunes" (Deuteronomy 30:2-3).

Obedience energizes, but a state of disobedience is fatiguing. Our soul becomes sluggish under the weight of going our own way. Disobedience is like swimming upstream in a raging river. It's like fighting against the wicked undertow of an ocean's crosscurrent. Life isn't designed to be lived in defiance to the will of the Lord. We're wired to walk with Him, not ignore Him or run away from Him. Turn down the heat of hate and become restored.

Forgive the sin and smile once again. You've probably been wronged, and you may not totally understand the extent of your hurt, so ask God to reveal how you hurt and where you need forgiveness. Start by asking God to forgive you, so you in turn can forgive others. It's lonely without the Lord's presence, wisdom, and blessing. Come back to Him for relational restoration.

Relish His restoration. Live to linger under the Lord's influence. Those restored are not bored.

―――∞∞∞―――

"Restore to me the joy of your salvation
and grant me a willing spirit, to
sustain me" (Psalm 51:12).

How can I express joy for the Lord's salvation? What does it mean for God to restore a willing spirit in me and to sustain me?

Related Readings
Psalm 41:3; Isaiah 57:18-19; Lamentations 5:21; Galatians 6:1;
1 Peter 5:10

45

Rich Affection

—∞∞∞—

Though your riches increase,
do not set your heart on them.

PSALM 62:10

M oney is a lover who romances us regularly. It seduces our emotions. It promises security though its outcome is uncertain. It promises satisfaction, but it's never content. It promises hope, but real hope is found in seeking first God's kingdom. It promises worldly wealth, but true riches belong to a growing relationship with Jesus. It promises a non-compete with Christ, but it's actually the number one competitor to our communion with Christ. It's a selfish lover.

Beware of the raw deal riches offer. Don't become seduced by the sirens of power and pride. We were saved by grace to get us to heaven, and we depend on grace to daily get us to God. We may have unique issues and opportunities due to having extra stuff. But an affection for riches can lead us to overindulge ourselves. Our loyalty can subtly shift from loving the Lord to loving stuff. So make sure extra things lead you into a deeper love relationship with the Giver—not the gifts. Jesus is very jealous.

—∞∞∞—

"Some people, eager for money, have wandered
from the faith and pierced themselves
with many griefs" (1 Timothy 6:10).

Wealth without a plan is irresponsible. A prayerful plan relegates money to a place of submission to God's ways. Begin engaging in a Bible study about money, and learn your role as a steward of God's stuff. Consider hiring a financial planner who can hold you accountable to stay fiscally pure to a kingdom paradigm of planning. Predetermine to be a predictable percentage giver. The Bible teaches the principle of steady plodding (Proverbs 21:5). Spontaneous giving is limited—mature giving has a guaranteed eternal return on investment.

Lead others to love the Lord instead of wealth. Be a role model to your children and peers. Trust God, not your wealth. Riches have never been true to those who trusted in them. They are themselves transient things and deserve our transient thoughts. Cleave to Christ, not to alluring riches that entangle and complicate your life. Jesus is the lover of your soul; place all your affection on Him and not on anything that will let you down. Don't fall in love with that which perishes, but with the One who keeps you from perishing. God is our rich affection!

"Set your hearts on things above, where Christ is seated at the right hand of God. Set your minds on things above, not on earthly things" (Colossians 3:1-2).

How can I grow my affection for Christ over cash? Why does my generosity dull my greed?

Related Readings
Proverbs 23:5; Ecclesiastes 5:10; Matthew 6:24,33; Luke 16:11

46

Earnest Seeker

⸎

You, God, are my God,
earnestly I seek you,
I thirst for you,
my whole being longs for you.

PSALM 63:1

God is ours because we are His. He's our personal God. He wants us to approach Him and address Him as "my God." This is what children do with their parents; they speak of "my mom" and "my dad." Parents are honored to be personally addressed by a loving and grateful child. This is how Christians are to approach their heavenly Father. We possess God because He possesses us. Possession breeds desire. Thus, we seek the Lord earnestly early in the day.

Earnest seekers of their Savior can't wait to be with Jesus. Early in the morning they want to encounter the love of God. Before the grassy dew is dried up from the sun's heat, they want to be lifted up by the warm love of the Lord. He removes any residue of worry from our soul. Like the chill of the morning, He takes away any fears that may have cooled our faith. Morning time with our Master is manna from heaven. God provides soul food for His children.

⸎

"Each morning everyone gathered as much [manna] as they needed, and when the sun grew hot, it melted away" (Exodus 16:21).

You may discover your weary soul is in a worrisome place. But weariness makes the presence of God more desirable. We become desperate for God when the fatigue of life parches our thirsty souls. When outward comforts are absent, we can press on as we walk with the inward serenity of our Savior Jesus. You may feel totally alone right now, because no one seems to understand. You feel under-appreciated. Learn how to love when you're not being loved. Learn how to serve when you're not being served. We earnestly seek God so we have energy to love others.

Earnest seekers know what to do when they find their heavenly Father. They rest. They reflect. They enjoy. They allow Him to rejuvenate their sickly soul. As you seek Him, you will find Him. When you find Him, allow Him to be your Father. Trust Him to love you as only He can. Trust Him to correct you as only He can. Trust Him to forgive you as only He can. Trust Him to lead you as only He can. Earnestly seek God, because He earnestly cares. Seekers enjoy satisfaction!

———— ∞ ————

"If...you seek the LORD your God, you will find him if you seek him with all your heart and with all your soul" (Deuteronomy 4:29).

How does the Lord want me to earnestly seek Him? What are the outcomes of coming to Christ?

Related Readings
Psalms 10:4; 24:6; Amos 5:14; Acts 17:27; Hebrews 11:6

47

Ponder and Proclaim

———— ⧼⧽ ————

All people will fear;
they will proclaim the works of God
and ponder what he has done.

PSALM 64:9

When we ponder God's works, we're compelled to proclaim them. His works are majestic because they call out praise to Him. God's works are displayed in the wonder of His creation. His signature is the soft, pure cloud, etched across the backdrop of a brilliant blue sky. His creativity cuts across all creation with unique varieties of plants and animals. However, His defining work is you. He created you for Himself—for His glory. You're an eternal emissary. You are your Father's child.

Therefore we ponder His work in us, which only begins at salvation. "He who began a good work in you will carry it on to completion until the day of Christ Jesus" (Philippians 1:6). Since our conversion to Christ, God has been at work in us. His work is to conform us into the likeness of His Son Jesus (Romans 8:29). We don't arrive until we get to heaven. Salvation is not an end in itself. God's profound and ongoing work is in and through us.

———— ⧼⧽ ————

"You make me glad by your deeds, Lord;
I sing for joy at what your hands
have done" (Psalm 92:4).

You're redeemed and forgiven by the grace of God (Ephesians 1:7).

You're a new creation in Christ (2 Corinthians 5:17). You're God's workmanship, created for good works (Ephesians 2:10). You're accepted by Christ (Romans 15:7). In Christ Jesus you have wisdom (1 Corinthians 1:30). You're joined to the Lord and are one spirit with Him (1 Corinthians 6:17). You're made complete in Christ (Colossians 2:10). Christ is your life (Colossians 3:4)!

After we ponder the work of God around us, in us, and through us, we're compelled to proclaim His faithfulness. Grateful mouths cannot keep shut. We thank Him quietly with a bowed head over meals. We announce His goodness by exercising good deeds for others. We exclaim obedience and loyalty to Him when we die daily to our own selfish desires and submit to His. The fear and love of God move us to ponder and proclaim God's grace. Proclaim the Lord with your life, and use words to spread the gospel of Jesus Christ!

"They tell of the power of your awesome works—
and I will proclaim your great deeds" (Psalm 145:6).

What works of God can I ponder in gratitude? What works of God will I boldly proclaim?

Related Readings
Psalms 66:5; 111:2; John 6:28; 1 Corinthians 12:6;
Philippians 2:13

48

Healthy Environments

⚬⚬⚬

You care for the land and water it;
you enrich it abundantly.
The streams of God are filled with water
to provide the people with grain,
for so you have ordained it.

PSALM 65:9

God created and cares for the earth. He softens the clouds and frees them to fill rivers with rain. The earth is the Lord's. Its fullness is for His glory. We sometimes harm the environment with senseless and shortsighted actions like littering, industrial waste, and horrific oil spills. Yet responsible followers of Jesus respect His natural resources. Environmental controls are right because they reflect wise stewardship of God's stuff. We have dominion over God's environment (Genesis 1:27-30) and so control our earthly environment.

In a similar way, law-abiding citizens in a free country control the environment in which they live. For example, who you spend time with determines who you become. "Do not be misled: Bad company corrupts good character" (1 Corinthians 15:33). You value what those closest to you value. If they model careless spending then you may soon discover yourself deep in debt. Don't take marriage advice from those who've had multiple marriages but didn't learn from their mistakes. Instead, value marriage environments of wisdom, love, fear of God, stability, and security.

⚬⚬⚬

"Whatever you have learned or received or heard from
me, or seen in me—put into practice" (Philippians 4:9).

God blesses environments that encourage engagement with Him. He's our ultimate keeper of environmental controls. Trust Him to lead you to the places that value what He values. Look for a spouse who loves Jesus more than he or she loves you. Pray for your spouse as you attend a Bible study group, serve in the church, or travel on mission trips. You can take the lead by creating environments of encouragement. Ask God to show you how to love those in your life.

Control your environment by creating your environment. The Holy Spirit working through you creates compelling places that invite others to Christ. The best environment is Christ-centric. Look therefore to the Lord. Trust Him. Expose yourself to healthy environments. Care about environmental controls. And, by God's grace, create environments that honor Christ!

—⊗⊗⊗—

"Walk with the wise and become wise,
for a companion of fools suffers harm" (Proverbs 13:20).

What changes do I need to make in the environments where I live, work, and play?

Related Readings
2 Chronicles 10:8; Proverbs 22:4-5; Acts 2:42; Hebrews 10:25

49

Sin Silences Prayer

*If I had cherished sin in my heart,
the Lord would not have listened.*

PSALM 66:18

Sin is a silencer that shoots down prayer. Our unconfessed sin cancels communion with Christ. It shatters the soul's longing for alignment with the Almighty. Sin over-promises and under-delivers. It promises pleasure, but its ultimate outcome is hollow. It promises freedom but leaves you in bondage. It promises privileges but takes them away.

Sin is suicide to your prayer life. Sin and your Savior cannot coexist. Sin is anti-Christ. We cannot harbor sin in our hearts and expect God in heaven to hear our prayers.

Sin confuses and complicates matters. Where there's confusion, look for unconfessed sin. We cannot hear God because sin has deafened our heart. The eardrums of our soul will burst under the pressure of unconfessed sin.

Sin also blocks the door of obedience. As it did with Cain, sin crouches at the door (Genesis 4:7) and hinders our way. Check your motives for coming to Christ in prayer. Make sure it's for His glory, not your own.

"When you ask, you do not receive, because you
ask with wrong motives, that you may spend
what you get on your pleasures" (James 4:3).

Marriage is particularly fertile ground for unconfessed sin to fester. Be on the lookout for sins that build barriers to intimacy with your spouse. It happens quickly in the rush to discipline children, or in the throes of making a living. We can easily become disconnected. This is why communication is critical in understanding which sins to confess and why. Husbands who take this lightly risk their prayers being unanswered. Humility leads to unhindered prayers.

Be assured the Lord listens and responds to prayers from a pure heart. He invites intimacy. He revels in restoring you into right relationship with Himself. His Spirit thrives in an unsoiled heart. Therefore prepare yourself with confession of sin before you ask anything of your Savior. Ask first for forgiveness from God and man, then go to God in prayerful petition. A pure heart is a prerequisite for supplications to your Savior. Purity positions you for intimate prayer.

"Husbands...be considerate as you live
with your wives...so that nothing will
hinder your prayers" (1 Peter 3:7).

What sin may be hindering my prayer life? Whose forgiveness do I need to seek?

Related Readings
Deuteronomy 1:45; 1 Samuel 8:18; Matthew 5:23-24; Colossians 3:19

50

God's Blessing Released

*May God be gracious to us and bless us
and make his face to shine on us—
so that your ways may be known on earth,
your salvation among all nations.*

PSALM 67:1-2

The mercy and grace of God govern His blessings. We shouldn't ask for the blessing of God until we receive forgiveness from God. We don't request the peace *of* God until we've made peace *with* God. We aren't invited onto the journey of God's blessing until we've first been born again.

Being born again gives us direct access to the beautiful blessings of our heavenly Father. He releases His blessing so we can be a blessing to all nations. We're a pass-through for blessings from God. Christ transforms us into an instrument of His blessing.

God blesses us to be a blessing to others. God wants to unleash His bountiful blessing—locally, regionally, nationally, and globally—through His children. If we hang on to His blessing just for ourselves, we risk losing it. The way we retain the blessing of the Lord is by giving it away. He expects His people to propagate His principles and precepts to all nations. Christ's blessing belongs in every tribe and tongue who trust Him.

"Therefore go and make disciples of
all nations" (Matthew 28:19).

Experiencing and imparting God's blessing will require uncommon faith. This elevated trust sees the face of God. His face shines on His faithful servants. It's a light that leads you to walk in the ways of your Lord. Common faith can see the deeds of God all around, but it's uncommon faith that *experiences* God. Uncommon faith sees the face of your heavenly Father, interprets His ways, discerns His plans, and in turn blesses others. We bless others so they'll enter into a relationship with the Blesser.

God's vast harvest is ready for the Lord's laborers; venture into it! Don't sit still waiting for the world to come to you. Go out by faith and overcome your fears. Trust God to keep you safe and healthy. Trust God to use you for His glory. You may go overseas to be a blessing, but you'll return home blessed. The revelation of Christ through your life may start a revolution of righteousness. Yes, be blessed to be a blessing!

"The LORD bless you
and keep you;
the LORD make his face shine on you
and be gracious to you;
the LORD turn his face toward you
and give you peace" (Numbers 6:24-26).

How has God blessed me over my lifetime? What's the purpose of Christ's blessings in my life?

Related Readings
Genesis 28:3; Deuteronomy 28:3-6; Psalms 28:9; 128:5;
John 4:35

51

Prodigal Fathers

———— ∞ ————

A father to the fatherless, a defender of widows,
is God in his holy dwelling.

PSALM 68:5

Prodigal fathers penetrate our society like rusty nails through a soft shoe. They're painful and poisonous. Pride drives them into irrational thinking and erratic behavior. Why do some men run away from their responsibilities as husband and dad? Could it be selfishness? No fear of God? No regard for right and wrong? Rebellion against the Almighty jettisons a person's faith. It may be a quiet, passive-aggressive rebellion, or it may be a boisterous rebellion. Foolish is the man who pursues fun over faith and family.

A prodigal wants the benefits of being an adult with the responsibility of a child. Some people spend a lifetime making excuses for not maturing. Why? It may be a hurt that has never healed. Wounded men wound others. Wounds without the balm of belief in God's grace never go away. Wounds build walls in relationships. Prodigal fathers are also angry. Their unresolved and conflicting emotions make them mad. It's in his desert of desperation that a man takes flight from his faith. Don't allow your desert to become a wilderness by deserting God.

———— ∞ ————

"He will turn the hearts of the parents
to their children, and the hearts of the
children to their parents" (Malachi 4:6).

If you're the recipient of a prodigal father's irresponsible actions, you have hope. You have a heavenly Father who cannot be tempted by evil (James 1:13). Your heavenly Father is there to love you and lead you into a deeper love relationship. Use this time of rejection to be accepted in the Beloved (Ephesians 1:6 KJV). Almighty God is never AWOL in His love relationship with you. Not only is He with you, He wants to serve you. Love? You have it. Wisdom? It's yours. Encouragement? Every day!

Pray about pursuing your prodigal father. Your presence reminds him of what God has for him. Christ in your life convicts him of who he needs to be, and what he needs to do. Inside your prodigal father is a scared and wounded animal in need of a gentle touch and healing. It's the Holy Spirit's work, through you and other believers, that will bring him to his knees. Keep the relationship robust for when he returns home. Your forgiveness fuels his faith!

"Forgive them, so that your Father in heaven
may forgive you your sins" (Mark 11:25).

Why is God's forgiveness based on me forgiving others? How can I express my forgiveness to my father?

Related Readings

Genesis 50:17; Exodus 22:22; Luke 1:17; 23:34; Titus 1:4;
1 John 5:1

52

Out of Control

⊶⊷

Save me, O God,
for the waters have come up to my neck.
I sink in the miry depths,
where there is no foothold.

PSALM 69:1-2

Like Jesus, we sometimes cry out to God, especially if we feel things are out of control. We cry out to Christ because we cannot get over our need for Him. We need to know He's in control. We need to know that what we're experiencing is being allowed by the Almighty. He knows what you're going through; He can be trusted to take care of you. God is in control. He's your hope, and He's your help.

It's the sinking feeling caused by oppressive circumstances that brings us the most consternation. Feeling totally out of control sends waves of fear over our faith. We sense we're drowning in despair. We gasp for God. In water we might swim, but in the mud and mire of being out of control, we seem helpless. We sink as if in quicksand. The more we struggle, the faster and deeper we descend.

Instead, we're to give our struggles over to our Savior Jesus. Be still so He can lift you up. Like Peter as he was sinking in the storm, we can cry out in our fears.

⊶⊷

"Lord, save me" (Matthew 14:30).

Your fervent prayers may have caused you to become hoarse from talking to heaven. Conversing with Christ has made your faith raw. Sometimes your eyes of faith fail you. They wander off your Lord to fixate on people and problems. Your eyes of faith fail when you lose focus on your heavenly Father.

In the world you have trouble; in Jesus you have peace (John 16:33). In the world you have discomfort; in Jesus you have comfort (2 Corinthians 1:3-6). In the world you have darkness; in Jesus you have light (John 9:5). In the world you have insecurity; Jesus makes you secure (1 John 5:13). In the world you have despair; Jesus brings hope (1 Peter 1:3). In the world you're defeated; in Jesus you've overcome (1 John 5:4-5). Sink in sin, or swim with Him!

"During the days of Jesus' life on earth, he offered up prayers and petitions with fervent cries and tears to the one who could save him from death, and he was heard because of his reverent submission" (Hebrews 5:7).

Where do my circumstances seem out of control? How can I more fully trust that Christ's hand governs these and all things?

Related Readings
Nehemiah 9:11; Psalm 32:6; Isaiah 43:2; Jonah 2:5; Luke 12:28

53

Hurry, God

But as for me, I am poor and needy;
come quickly to me, O God.
You are my help and my deliverer;
LORD, do not delay.

PSALM 70:5

Adversity invites a sense of urgency. We're urgent in our need for God. We're urgent for reassurance of God's presence and relief from our stressful situation. We're urgent for help from heaven. In our prayers we cry out to Christ. We plead with Him to take away our pain. This is the nature of the needy. We need God. So out of our pain, our prayers shout for something from our Savior. We need to know He's near—we need to know now. We pray, "Lord, do not delay."

In poverty of spirit we see our greatest need for God. In our weakness we're most teachable toward God's wisdom. Our spiritual eyes are clearly focused on our utter dependence on Christ. In God's economy, our poverty becomes our wealth (Revelation 2:9) and our weakness becomes our strength (Hebrews 11:34).

"That is why, for Christ's sake, I delight in
weaknesses, in insults, in hardships, in
persecutions, in difficulties. For when I am
weak, then I am strong" (2 Corinthians 12:10).

However, what took years to incur may take years to dig out of. A crisis is Christ's opportunity to share with you His "true riches" (Luke 16:11). He'll make haste to walk with you through your mess. His presence is your best prescription during times of illness. Your heavenly Father is your provider. His principles work. In sickness, use this opportunity of humility to seek others who are healthy. Let them mentor you through their experience.

Maintain a sense of urgency for the Lord at all times. In reality, we're always in desperate need of Him. Dependence on God isn't conditional on a crisis. Our requirement for walking with Jesus is our ability to breathe. Maintain motivation for your Master without having to experience pain first. Before pain comes, we can still fervently pray and seek Him. The good times require God as much as the bad times. Be quick to call on Him while things are still calm. Prayerful preparation averts panic in a future crisis. Ask Christ to come quickly to you.

How can I increase the intensity of my dependence on Christ?

Related Readings
Psalm 141:1; Acts 3:19; 1 Corinthians 1:27; Revelation 1:8; 22:20

54

Womb to Tomb

⎯⎯∞⎯⎯

From birth I have relied on you;
you brought me forth from my mother's womb.
I will ever praise you…
Even when I am old and gray,
do not forsake me, my God.

PSALM 71:6,18

From our mother's womb to our final tomb, we have opportunities to trust God. As an infant we're unaware of our 100 percent dependence on Him, but we grow to understand this over time. It began making sense when we prayed as a child, "God is great, God is good, let us thank Him for our food." There was a childlike trust that had no issue with the vastness of God's power and influence. He was and is our Savior from our sins. Christ is our confidence.

Once we graduate from those early days of faith exploration, we're commanded to pass on to our progeny the ways of God. As parents, we're to bring up our children in the "training and instruction of the Lord" (Ephesians 6:4). Mom and Dad are to guide and teach their children. It's sobering to think we represent the Lord to our little ones. This is why we pray together as parents for our sons and daughters. Remembering God as a young person can bring fulfillment as an older person.

⎯⎯∞⎯⎯

"Remember your Creator
in the days of your youth" (Ecclesiastes 12:1).

Youth well spent is a comfort in old age. You have joyful reflection.

There are limited regrets when you go with God. Yes, growing old possesses its own set of unique challenges. The beauty of your youth begins to bow to the aging process. Your body becomes a burden to your mind. However, don't allow declining eyesight to keep you from seeing God. The need for glasses, surgery, or doctors is what happens with these temporary tents we live within.

Our strength decays, we walk slower, but Christ is our strength—and His pace is perfect. Our mature mind begins to forget names and places. It becomes hard to recollect where we've been. But it's important that we age well by exchanging the temporal with the eternal. We substitute stubbornness with sensitivity. We replace peevishness with patience. We exchange fear for faith. Instead of lamenting our infirmities, we praise God for the gift of another day. We leverage our gray hair for God. Teach others to trust Him from the womb to the tomb.

———◦∞◦———

"Even to your old age and gray hairs
I am he, I am he who will sustain you" (Isaiah 46:4).

What does it look like to have childlike trust? When the time comes, how can I leverage my gray hair for God?

Related Readings
Psalms 18:35; 119:117; Ecclesiastes 11:8; 2 Timothy 1:5; 2:22

55

Children of the Needy

*May he defend the afflicted among the people
and save the children of the needy.*

PSALM 72:4

The children of the needy are in need, though often their needs sit in somber silence until they cry out for attention. There's nothing that tugs more at the heart than a deprived little one. They didn't choose their pitiful plight any more than the progeny of the privileged chose theirs.

It could be the parents of the needy are just getting by. Or perhaps a single parent is struggling in survival mode. Regardless, our loving Lord defends the afflicted and saves the children of the needy.

Sometimes divorce creates needy children. They're conflicted between Mom and Dad. What began as a heavenly home of support has become a hellish one of selfishness. Neediness engulfs offspring caught in the crossfire of a caustic divorce. Broken marriages break the hearts of children. They suffer the most, though they're the least responsible for the shattered vows. While Mom and Dad try to get their act together, innocent children look to get their needs met. They may find love in the right places, like church and Christian homes, or they may look elsewhere.

*"I will contend with those who contend with you,
and your children I will save"* (Isaiah 49:25).

The children of the needy cannot be ignored. Jesus modeled this.

"Let the little children come to me, and do not hinder them, for the kingdom of heaven belongs to such as these" (Matthew 19:14). Needy children cannot be neglected. Maybe we're blessed with healthy children, so we can reach out to unhealthy ones. Is there a teenager in your life who's currently disconnected from both parents? He or she needs a safe environment of liberating love. Rebellion subsides under a roof of warm relationships. Your home is a haven of hospitality for the needy; invite them in!

Look for ways to love children of the needy. Invest in their education. Take them to church so they can hear the love of Jesus and be loved. Encourage laughter and comfort their tears. Let them be children, so they can become children. Children who lose trust in adults have difficulty trusting Christ—so stay trustworthy. Be a bridge for their beliefs.

Expose your own children to the needy so they'll develop gratitude and a heart for service. Follow Christ's example by looking for a child to love, to defend, and to rescue from unrighteousness.

———— ∞ ————

"Pharaoh's daughter...named him Moses, saying,
'I drew him out of the water' " (Exodus 2:10).

What needy child needs my attention and help? How can I teach my child to serve the needy?

Related Readings
Job 24:3-11; Ecclesiastes 4:13-14; Matthew 18:3; Mark 9:37

56

Perplexed but Poised

*Surely God is good to Israel,
to those who are pure in heart.
But as for me, my feet had almost slipped;
I had nearly lost my foothold.*

PSALM 73:1-2

God can be perplexing. Because His ways are so much larger in scope, our lack of understanding can push us to the verge of losing hope. We don't understand why our good God isn't giving immediate relief to our pain or to the suffering we see others experiencing.

When we're uncertain, that's the time to confess our need for Christ. Purity of heart paves the way during perplexing times. We need the Lord most when our faith is least. Purity facilitates clarity. We keep our soul poised in prayer.

Life can be perplexing. Why did your friend say one thing and do another? Why do you always seem to face financial pressure? Why are your parents consumed with themselves? Why are your teenagers disengaged and distant? Why does work seem like a dead-end road? Nagging questions tug at your heart and cause you to doubt. Allow your doubts to drive you toward God, not away from Him. It's in your perplexity that you pray to your perfect God for His will to be done. His integrity is intact. He's your good and gracious Savior.

"We are hard pressed on every side, but not crushed; perplexed, but not in despair" (2 Corinthians 4:8).

Perplexity is not sin. Just because you're perplexed with something outside your control doesn't mean you're at fault. But it's a warning to watch out for temptation. "Be careful that you don't fall!" (1 Corinthians 10:12). Guard your thoughts. You cannot prevent a bird from flying over your head, but you can keep him from making a nest in your hair. Take every thought captive in obedience to Christ (2 Corinthians 10:5).

Saturate your mind with truth so it flushes out the fear and lies that torment your trust in the Lord. Perplexity is part of your walk with Jesus. Stay poised by faith. Don't allow your bewilderment to become spiritual vertigo. Keep your balance by believing. Your Savior keeps you from slipping, your heavenly Father keeps you from falling, and the Holy Spirit supports you. Perplexity is your opportunity to joyfully trust and obey.

"We know that in all things God works for the good of those who love him" (Romans 8:28).

How can I keep my soul poised during perplexing times? Why is my purity of heart important?

Related Readings
Daniel 4:19; Psalm 40:2; Acts 2:12; Galatians 4:18-20

57

Feeling Rejected

O God, why have you rejected us forever?
Why does your anger smolder against
the sheep of your pasture?

PSALM 74:1

As recipients of God's righteous anger we may feel rejected, even though His anger is directed toward our disobedience, not us. He still loves us as His children when we drift from His best. Sometimes in our fear or frivolity we flee from His influence. Or more subtly and subconsciously, we may daily drift in the wrong direction. This is terrible terrain because it's void of the blessing of God. Venturing away from the Almighty is unwise. Sheep need their shepherd.

Jesus is the Shepherd of your soul. He's the "great Shepherd" (Hebrews 13:20). Good shepherds see to it that their sheep are properly fed, watered, and protected from the elements. They care for them, because they care. When a sheep strays from the flock, it startles the shepherd into action. Once they're found, there's relief, but not without anger for their having strayed. Anger over self-inflicted harm comes from love. God's wrath is real. His anger is for our protection.

"You are a forgiving God, gracious and compassionate,
slow to anger and abounding in love. Therefore
you did not desert them" (Nehemiah 9:17).

The anger of loved ones can be seen as evidence of something gone wrong. Don't write off the emotional outburst of another as someone who has no self-control. Good anger is a safety valve for the soul. Be grateful when those who love you confront you. Your pride will take offense, but your humility will be teachable. Listen to criticism and see it as your accountability. Develop the heart of a child, the mind of a student, and the hide of a rhinoceros. Constructive anger respects the person but rejects bad behavior.

Be grateful that God gets mad. It's wise to fear His reaction to our unwise actions. Flee from every foolish habit; if you have to sneak around to do it, that should tell you something. Can you imagine where we might be if our fear of God didn't throttle back our bad behavior? See God's anger from the lens of love; see its warm acceptance of you, its cold rejection of sinful attitudes and actions. See righteous indignation as a wake-up call from Christ!

"So he made a whip out of cords, and drove all
from the temple courts, both sheep and cattle;
he scattered the coins of the money changers
and overturned their tables" (John 2:15).

By God's grace, how can I receive another's anger and become better, not defensive?

Related Readings
Hosea 14:4; Joel 2:13; Jonah 4:2; Ephesians 4:26; James 1:20

58

God Promotion

No one from the east or the west
or from the desert can exalt themselves.
It is God who judges:
He brings one down, he exalts another.

PSALM 75:6-7

Sometimes we strive unnecessarily to seek promotion. We forget that heaven handles this responsibility. Joseph discovered this when he went from the pit of death to the palace of power (Genesis 39). This doesn't lessen our commitment to excellence and hard work, but it does help us lean hard into the Lord. He's our promoter, our agent for advancement. Allow Christ to be your champion. The timing of our advancement is ordained in heaven, not on earth.

Pray to your advocate Jesus. Talk with Him about His role and your responsibility. Like the owner who gave responsibility to three managers while he was away, God does have expectations of your efforts (Matthew 25). The providence of God doesn't mean you're passive. You're called to do excellent work with the motive of glorifying God. Focus on giving Him credit for your accomplishments, and He may entrust you with more responsibility. The quality of your work and relationships is a reflection on Jesus. He looks for those He can lift up for His own glory.

"All those who exalt themselves will be
humbled, and those who humble themselves
will be exalted" (Luke 14:11).

A premature promotion can be perilous. Some who arrive too soon are sent back to the beginning to learn valuable lessons. So use any parenthesis of time before you're promoted to prepare your character. New responsibilities may require more intense integrity and a deep reservoir of faith. Stay focused on faith development, and leave the opening and closing of doors to divine discretion. Let the Lord bring opportunity beckoning. Promotion in God's timing is best for all.

Above all else, don't miss God in the midst of your motivation for advancement. He'll give you the people, passion, and provisions for your new role. Moses had Aaron. David had Jonathan. Peter and John had each other. Paul had Barnabas, Silas, Timothy, and others at various times.

Promotion is a platform to love people with the Lord. Love them, so they will love Him. Here's where God's blessings intersect in people's lives. Give Christ credit, and He'll give you influence with those you lead.

———∞———

"Wealth and honor come from you;
you are the ruler of all things.
In your hands are strength and power
to exalt and give strength to all" (1 Chronicles 29:12).

What work of grace does God want to prepare in my heart, so I'm ready for work advancement?

Related Readings
Psalm 90:17; Isaiah 64:8; Luke 10:40; Acts 20:35

59

Reflection of God

⚮

You are radiant with light,
more majestic than mountains rich with game.

PSALM 76:4

Followers of Jesus are reflections of Jesus. This is who we are. Just as the moon is a reflection of the sun, we are reflections of the Son. His beam of light blankets our lives like the sun's reflective rays on a sunbather on a hot summer day. God created light (Genesis 1:3), and He invites us to walk in the greater light of His love. So focus on being like Jesus; don't be driven by doing for Jesus. Like a full moon, a life that reflects the Lord draws people's attention.

It's when we're in right relationship with our heavenly Father that we're right for reflection. He lights up a life that's submitted to Him. The lampshade of sin is removed when we confess to Christ our desperate dependence on Him. Because we're in Christ, we're in the light. We shine because our Savior shines through us. Light is translucent. It reflects best off holiness. Character ignites the light of the Lord to reach into the darkest crevices of our world. You are the light of the Lord.

⚮

"For you were once darkness, but now you are light in the Lord. Live as children of the light (for the fruit of the light consists in all goodness, righteousness and truth) and find out what pleases the Lord" (Ephesians 5:8-10).

When we forgive, we reflect Jesus. When we care, we reflect Christ.

When we cry over the condition of Christless souls, we reflect what our Lord experienced when He wept over the lost condition of His people (Luke 19:41-42). When we feed the hungry, clothe the naked, administer medical care to the sick, and house the homeless, we reflect Jesus. When we speak a word of encouragement, we reflect Christ. Reflecting God means we resolve to be who we are in Christ.

Lead others into the light of the Lord. Use your home to illuminate His love. Your home can become a little bit of heaven to those whose lives are a lot like hell. Invest time and money in those who cannot or will not give back. Orphans, single parents, the jobless, the homeless, homosexuals, adulterers, divorcees, and the poor all need the warmth of God's love. So reflect God to them. Be a responsible citizen in the kingdom of light!

"The Father...has qualified you to share in
the inheritance of his holy people in the
kingdom of light" (Colossians 1:12).

How can I reflect Jesus in my conversations and my actions?

Related Readings
Psalm 4:6; Isaiah 2:5; 60:1; Acts 13:47-48; Philippians 2:14-15

60

A Good Memory

―――――∞∞∞――――――

*I will remember the deeds of the L*ORD*;*
yes, I will remember your miracles of long ago.
I will consider all your works
and meditate on all your mighty deeds.

PSALM 77:11-12

A good memory makes for a faithful follower of Jesus. It's good when our soul thinks back and reflects on His faithfulness. When we become shortsighted in our faith, we struggle and become stressed out.

Good memories remind us of God's goodness. His track record can be trusted. You may be experiencing a famine of faith, but you can still draw on the storehouse of stories that illustrate the past works of God.

Beware of short-term memory loss in your trust of the Lord. Even Jesus's disciples wrestled with this (Matthew 16:9).

A good memory brings to remembrance God's good deeds. Remember when He redirected your life from a disastrous outcome to one filled with peace and hope. He bought you with the price of His precious Son Jesus. This is a majestic memory of switching masters. Now your allegiance is to Almighty God. Your memory may bring back prayers He has answered, people who've come to Christ, or conversations with other Christ followers. Jesus said to remember His words. His words woo us back when we wander away.

―――――∞∞∞――――――

"Remember what I told you" (John 15:20).

The art of meditation brings back good memories. Meditation

makes for rich talk. A mind that doesn't meditate is like dilapidated machinery corroded with rust. Conversations without contemplation are barren of substance. Meditation makes for more meaningful talk. Write out what He says so you can filter your thinking into pure words and phrases not easily forgotten. Remember the Lord's Word and His works!

Avoid filling your mind with useless information. Don't mentally replay your regrets and wishful thinking. What's done is done; nothing can change what has happened. Obsessing over bad memories builds bitterness and betrays your freedom in Christ. Forget your former life of pain, and focus on what you've gained with God. Forget your former life of unprincipled living, and embrace your new life in Christ. By God's grace, make new memories with Him!

"But now that you know God—or rather are known by God—how is it that you are turning back to those weak and miserable forces? Do you wish to be enslaved by them all over again?" (Galatians 4:9).

What memories of God's good works and words do I need to meditate on?

Related Readings
Numbers 15:40; Deuteronomy 7:18; Psalm 22:27; Luke 17:32; 2 Corinthians 9:6

61

Listen to Learn

———∞∞∞———

O my people, hear my teaching;
listen to the words of my mouth.

PSALM 78:1

Students of Jesus listen to learn. They listen to Him and to those He brings into their lives. When we're listening in order to learn, we move closer to the Lord and others. This is why we give earnest attention to what He says. We hear the Almighty and act on His words. Obedience is a sign of effective listening. Wise is the man or woman who listens well to the Lord. Jesus spoke as one with authority and people listened (Matthew 7:28-29). Wisdom listens and learns.

The habit of not listening can get us into trouble. But there's a deeper level of listening that engages our heart around eternal issues. It focuses on the principles of Scripture for the purpose of making a life. In listening to learn, we're motivated to understand the context of Christ's teaching. Jesus said, "Learn from me" (Matthew 11:29). A first step in learning to listen is obeying. Because Christ learned obedience from suffering, so can we.

———∞∞∞———

"Son though he was, he learned obedience
from what he suffered" (Hebrews 5:8).

Our listening and learning must also extend to people. God has lessons for us to learn from almost everyone we come in contact with. But we'll miss this instruction if we don't listen intently to them. We show love to others when we listen. Wisdom values everyone's instruction. Listen to others with the same undivided attention you give to God. Don't be slow to learn. Slow down your spirit and focus on the moment. Have clear comprehension with an eye to application.

Once you've listened and learned, pass on your valuable lessons to others. The best teachers are excellent listeners. They don't just transfer information; transformation is the outcome of their teaching. Teachers who listen well are much better prepared to teach well. You pass on your "learning from listening" to those who are eager to listen and learn.

Listen well and learn more easily. Be quick to listen, and you'll be fast to learn!

"It is hard to make it clear to you because you
no longer try to understand" (Hebrews 5:11).

How can I listen in a way that honors the Lord? What is God trying to teach me?

Related Readings

Deuteronomy 4:10; Jeremiah 12:16-17; Matthew 11:28-30;
1 Timothy 5:4

62

Suffering and Seeking

———✸———

Whenever God slew them, they would seek him;
they eagerly turned to him again.

PSALM 78:34

Suffering has the tendency to shake us into seeking the Lord. When we become uncomfortable in our circumstances, we long for the Lord. Christ becomes our interest when our interests are interrupted. It's not a bad thing when suffering sends us to our Savior. We knew Him in our salvation, but we didn't know Him in our suffering. Suffering moves us beyond the surface with our Savior to an intense level of loving intimacy and dependence. In our own sufferings we come to understand what it's like to share in His sufferings (Philippians 3:10).

We tend to obey when we resonate with the rod of God's reproof. He disciplines us when we get out of line (Hebrews 12:5-11). Because He loves us, He longs for us to seek Him with all our heart. It's a passionate desire for unhindered intimacy.

Our suffering gets our eyes off ourselves and onto Him. Suffering delivers us from self to our Savior. In our suffering we see Christ clearly. Don't pity yourself by staying stuck on yourself, but throw yourself into the arms of your heavenly Father who loves you.

———✸———

"I would still have this consolation—
my joy in unrelenting pain—
that I had not denied the words of
the Holy One" (Job 6:10).

By faith we cast our burdens on God. The sharp stabs of suffering awaken the memories of His faithfulness. When our prideful props are knocked away, we're positioned for total dependence on the Lord. Maybe your career has gone south—then go hard after Him. Or you've become soft on sin—go hard after Him. You have been treated unfairly—go hard after Him. Maybe your anger has the best of you—go hard after Him. You are bankrupt—go hard after Him. Use this time of suffering to seek your Savior.

Suffering brought about by the Lord's discipline is for our good so we may share in His holiness. It's painful now, but it produces a harvest of righteousness. Holiness means He has all of us. Leverage your suffering for the sake of others. See God in your suffering so you won't stay angry. Move toward the Lord and be glad!

"God disciplines us for our good, in order that
we may share in his holiness" (Hebrews 12:10).

How does the Lord want me to use my suffering to seek His heart?

Related Readings
Psalm 42:10-11; Acts 3:18-19; 1 Thessalonians 5:9; 1 Peter 2:20

63

Empowering Leadership

———∞∞———

David shepherded them with integrity of heart;
with skillful hands he led them.

PSALM 78:72

Leadership can be daunting, even overwhelming. You may lack experience in a new area, so admit your shortcomings and be open and honest about your need for the team's expertise. It's better to release our inexperience up front than to hide or ignore it until it reveals itself. Leaders with integrity know what they can and cannot do well. They look to others to shore up their weakness, and they serve others out of their strengths. You can be educated without having to become an expert. Indeed, integrity is always learning from other gifted leaders.

Leaders who empower lead out of a position of humility. This means they have more questions than answers. They help other team members discover the best answers. They're the CQA (Chief Question Asker). They're skilled at harvesting everyone's best thinking and converging diverse ideas into the best answer. The direct approach may get results sooner. Dictating what to do can be more efficient, but lacks sustainability. It's wiser to go through a process of debate and buy-in. Collective thinking from the whole produces the best outcomes.

———∞∞———

"The advice Ahithophel gave was like that of
one who inquires of God" (2 Samuel 16:23).

Ask God for wisdom to understand what questions to ask, and for patience to pause for another's answer. It's in our waiting that God makes leaders out of followers. Followers who fail to think stay stunted in their leadership, while followers who learn to think grow their leadership capacity. They can eventually surpass their leader's leadership. You want to work yourself out of a job. Wise and patient leaders grow a team that surpasses their capacity.

Skilled leaders are able to discern those who don't have the capability to grow as leaders. They may not have the character to handle leadership's demands. Expel team members of bad character, or they'll corrupt the whole. Their bad motives may be as obvious and loud as a rattlesnake, or they may be as quiet and deceptive as a water moccasin; either way, they're a threat.

Some team members may have the character but not the competence to grow into leaders. Skilled leaders of integrity value everyone. Above all, they follow the Lord's leadership.

"May integrity and uprightness protect me,
because my hope, LORD, is in you" (Psalm 25:21).

How can I help develop leadership in others? What evidence is there that I follow the Lord well?

Related Readings
Genesis 17:1; Proverbs 22:29; Ecclesiastes 2:19; Matthew 22:16; Titus 2:7

64

Desperate Need

———— ⚭ ————

May your mercy come quickly to meet us,
for we are in desperate need.
Help us, God our Savior.

PSALM 79:8-9

Everyone's in desperate need of God. There are no exemptions. The rich and the poor desperately need God. The educated and the ignorant desperately need God. The respected and disrespected desperately need God. The wise and the foolish desperately need God. We're desperately needy because we cannot save ourselves. In and of ourselves, we have no hope. Our desperation graduates to despair if we stay there. Yes, humility stays needy for the Holy Spirit.

In Christ we have a living hope that meets our every need. Only when we acknowledge our desperate need for Christ are we ready to receive His grace. For some, unfortunately, it takes a crisis to awaken their desperate need for Jesus. They slumber away in their sin-sedated state, only tipping God with trivial pursuit. Or they find fulfillment in other respected places like family, work, or community service. But our interests, however narcissistic or noble, cannot substitute for our desperate need for God's goodness and mercy to lead our lives.

———— ⚭ ————

"My God will meet all your needs according to the
riches of his glory in Christ Jesus" (Philippians 4:19).

Because of our desperate need for Christ, we can rejoice. We're full of joy because we know Jesus is our Savior and Lord. Because our Redeemer lives, we can face tomorrow. Our desperate need leads us to the Lord. This is where we find peace and patience. Self-sufficiency will try to slither its way into our thinking as we experience success. Our success, however, just means a greater need for God. Accolades can lure us into kingdom irrelevance if we aren't utterly abandoned to Christ. Humility keeps us desperate for Jesus.

We're all desperately needy for God, so there's no room for pride. We're all beggars who have the opportunity to share the bread of God's grace with each other. It's in the rawness of our needy condition that we have the opportunity to model dependence and total trust. We're sheep in need of a shepherd. With Him we're wise and confident. Without Him we're confused and lost. Desperate dependence on Christ within leads to a quiet confidence without. When we're desperately needy, we become radically loved by the Lord!

—◦≈◦—

"Once more the humble will rejoice in the LORD;
the needy will rejoice in the Holy
One of Israel" (Isaiah 29:19).

Why is it important to stay needy for Jesus? What keeps me desperate for God?

Related Readings
Psalms 60:3; 142:6; Jeremiah 20:13; Lamentations 2:19; John 7:37-39

65

New Opportunity

You transplanted a vine from Egypt...
You cleared the ground for it,
and it took root and filled the land.

PSALM 80:8-9

Sometimes we need a new opportunity. We need to challenge our career path. We need to further our faith. We need to nurture the soil of our soul. God knows our need to conquer new goals and grow closer to Him. We remained faithful during the downturn, but now circumstances have somewhat stabilized. We may be like a star athlete who has performed well for a season, but a trade to a different team is what's best for everyone. It's time to transition. Transition requires trust. We celebrate what Christ has done through us, and now we move on by faith.

You've managed well what God has given you, and now He's opening up another door of opportunity. God has nurtured your life like a small branch, and has prepared it to be vibrant and healthy. God has cared for you, so you can care for others. Healthy vines produce firm branches with luscious fruit. God wants to plant you in this new opportunity where the soil is fertile. He has prepared this next season for your roots to go deep and wide for the kingdom of God.

"No branch can bear fruit by itself; it must remain in the vine. Neither can you bear fruit unless you remain in me" (John 15:4).

However, don't allow change to hurt your relationship with Christ. A new opportunity probably requires more time with Jesus. Discomfort is sometimes necessary to shake us out of our comfort zone and cause us to cling to Christ. Newness gives us fresh appreciation and motivation. It may be a new church or neighborhood. A new boyfriend or girlfriend. It may be a new hobby or a move to another continent. Embrace the new with fresh faith in God!

Receive by faith whatever new opportunity awaits you, and don't look back. Israel stayed confused when they looked back and second-guessed their exodus from Egypt (Numbers 14:3-4). Stay focused ahead on what Almighty God has for you next. Out on the limb with Jesus is the location of the best fruit. Steward it well, and He'll expand His influence through you. Move forward by faith. Don't look back with regret, as Lot's wife did (Genesis 19:26). New beginnings begin with trust in Jesus.

"By faith Abraham, when called to go…obeyed
and went, even though he did not know
where he was going" (Hebrews 11:8).

What new opportunity is God calling me to follow? What fruit does Christ want to bear in me?

Related Readings
Proverbs 27:25-27; Isaiah 43:19; Acts 10:19-21; Hebrews 11:6

66

Listen Well

Hear me, my people, and I will warn you—
if you would only listen to me, Israel!

PSALM 81:8

S ometimes we listen only to what we want to hear. If we drift into this spiritually insensible state, we become deaf to God. Are Christ's commands falling on deaf ears? The sign language of our Savior may be signaling us back to His love and care. Jesus taught the wisdom of listening to God. He said in John 6:45, "It is written in the Prophets: 'They will all be taught by God.' Everyone who has heard the Father and learned from him comes to me." An educational exchange with eternity draws us closer to Christ. The Holy Spirit is our teacher.

Listening lures us to the Lord. Like attractive bait in front of a hungry fish, our heavenly Father hooks us with truth. He often uses godly messengers to get across His personalized message. In actively listening to the Almighty's ambassadors, we gain discernment into what to do or not to do. Your spouse, teacher, parents, pastor, and godly friends may well speak on behalf of your Savior. Other voices can seem louder and more persuasive, but listen to those who love you—who want God's best for you.

"We are from God, and whoever knows God listens
to us; but whoever is not from God does not
listen to us. This is how we recognize the Spirit of
truth and the spirit of falsehood" (1 John 4:6).

If you continue down the road of resistance to Spirit-led listening, then God may give you over to your desires. He doesn't waste His time with those who won't adhere to His words. He doesn't cast the pearls of His wisdom among stubborn swine (Matthew 7:6). He shares with those who steward well what they hear, understand, and do. The Lord longs to engage your heart through the stability of Scripture. His Word communicates truth. Listen...learn...live!

Listen well in your encounters with Christ. Look for His pensive and pure voice through those who love Him. Selective listening is smart only if it ignores lies and stays sensitive to God. Turn down the volume on the Christless culture which constantly cries out for conformation to its creeds. Only one voice rightly demands your undivided attention: Almighty God's. Therefore be selective by listening well to what your Savior says. His words are sweet as honey to the soul!

---∞---

"My sheep listen to my voice; I [Jesus] know
them, and they follow me" (John 10:27).

How can I better listen to the Lord? What is the Holy Spirit saying to my soul?

Related Readings
1 Samuel 8:7; Malachi 2:2; 1 Corinthians 14:21; Revelation 2:7

67

God Presides

God presides in the great assembly;
he renders judgment among the "gods."

PSALM 82:1

God presides over the courtroom of our culture. He's the Chief Justice over our cares, concerns, and corruption. Nothing done in this life sneaks by our Savior. We can be certain that Christ will judge our actions and our inactions. He's the judge to be feared. He's the judge our judges should fear.

For Moses, God was his model of justice as he sat in judgment of the people. They stood to plead their case while he sat, listened, and dispensed wisdom (Exodus 18:13).

The judges of our land are not the final answer. They answer to Almighty God. Woe to them if they acquit the guilty or condemn the innocent. Great responsibility resides with the one who presides in judgment. Pray therefore for our judges to petition heaven for help. There's a guide for defining right and wrong. The Bible is the basis for our judicial system. Holy Scripture is the baseline for our laws. It defines and illustrates God's moral law. It's designed to be the conscience of our culture. Judges have boundaries to prevent them from perverting justice.

"Select capable men from all the people—
men who fear God, trustworthy men who
hate dishonest gain... Have them serve as
judges for the people" (Exodus 18:21-22).

The same applies when we find ourselves in a position to preside over another's problems. Two parties may bring to us conflicting opinions. Our first question as mediator is, what does the Bible teach? What eternal principles apply to this situation? A child may be right in their grievance against their parents, but are they honoring them (Ephesians 6:1-2) in the process? We use our level of influence to leverage what the Lord thinks. Engage conflict with Christ's view.

Live your life with actions that can stand the scrutiny of your Savior. Be ever aware of the courtroom of Christ as your ultimate accountability (1 Corinthians 3:11-13). You may mask your motives with a smile, but your true intent will one day be exposed. The Lord God is your final authority. What you do in the dark—where no one's watching— will one day come out under the light of the Lord. Live an accountable life that will one day answer to God.

"The Lord...will bring to light what is hidden
in darkness and will expose the motives
of the heart" (1 Corinthians 4:5).

Do I trust the Lord as the ultimate judge? What motives of mine does the Spirit need to purify?

Related Readings
Psalms 7:8; 9:4; Proverbs 31:9; Matthew 7:1-2; Romans 2:1; 1 Peter 4:17

68

Shamed into Seeking

Cover their faces with shame, LORD,
so that they will seek your name.

PSALM 83:16

Shame can be a catalyst for seeking Christ. It's in our shame that we're positioned to seek the Lord. Our shameful state opens the door to our Savior Jesus. You may have been caught stealing, lying, or flirting with another person's spouse. Your drinking may have become excessive, or your prescription drug use lingered too long. Your gossip got the best of you. Your irresponsible actions have come to light. You're embarrassed—even ashamed. What should you do?

We can be relieved that our shameful indiscretions can give us a new lease with the Lord. Shame is meant to wean us from our idols and set us on the path of pursuing Christ. In our most embarrassing moments we need to remember the love and acceptance of our heavenly Father. The mind can label something as shameful that the heart embraces as delightful. God's fame covers sin's shame, as it did for the prodigal son who came to his senses and sought forgiveness from the one he'd sinned against (Luke 15:17-19).

"May I wholeheartedly follow your decrees,
that I may not be put to shame" (Psalm 119:80).

There's no level of shameful sin that Christ cannot cleanse. So seek God while He can be found. You may be ashamed for not appropriating

His grace sooner, but you won't be ashamed for calling on His name now. Speak the name of Jesus. It soothes your shame and satisfies your soul. His name is wonderful. His name is beautiful. Jesus is above every name; at His name we'll all one day bow in unfettered and shameless worship (Philippians 2:9-11).

Therefore awaken from your shameful slumber. The constant correction in your conscience is from Christ. He loves you too much to leave you in your shameful state. Renew your mind (Romans 12:2) from any temporary amnesia to the Almighty's way of doing things. Shameful and alarming are the ways of the world; peaceful and content are the ways of God. So don't be ashamed to seek the Lord. Seek Him while He may be found. Seek Him now while it matters. Be ever present in prayerful petition. Shame is His means to seeking Him!

"Hope does not put us to shame, because God's love
has been poured out into our hearts through the
Holy Spirit, who has been given to us" (Romans 5:5).

Why does God's fame cover sin's shame? How can I seek the Lord in a way that protects me from shameful regrets?

Related Readings
Psalm 69:6; Romans 1:25-27; 9:33; 1 Corinthians 1:27;
2 Corinthians 4:2

69

God's Gatekeeper

*Better is one day in your courts
than a thousand elsewhere;
I would rather be a doorkeeper in the house of my God
than dwell in the tents of the wicked.*

PSALM 84:10

We are God's gatekeepers. We're the gatekeepers of His truth. We're the gatekeepers of His trust, His time, and His grace. A gatekeeper for God is larger than life. It's better to have a lowly position with the Lord than a glamorous role without Him. A gatekeeper gets to see what's inside. We get a glimpse of God. Jesus is our gate to God. He's our passage from pride's grip into the humble hands of heaven.

A day as God's gatekeeper is more valuable and interesting than a thousand days somewhere exotic but without eternal consequences. You can travel around the world in 80 days, but in a moment—through meditation and prayer—you can make a pilgrimage to heaven. The tents of the wicked are adventurous and inviting, but in the end they're at the mercy of the world's elements. Exposed to evil influences, the tents of the wicked travel like lost nomads.

"I [Jesus] am the gate; whoever enters
through me will be saved" (John 10:9).

The house of the Lord is full of hope. It's stable and dependable. The pillars of God's character rest on the foundation of His faithfulness. His house is forever accessible by faith. Jesus didn't have an earthly home to lay His head (Luke 9:58), but He had a heavenly home to rest His heart. Therefore relish the opportunity to be God's gatekeeper. Show up to serve, and see what He has in store. God's worst is better than the devil's best.

There may be times when the Lord seems to have gone away—like the entrepreneur traveling on business, leaving his stewards to manage his money resourcefully (Matthew 25:14-30). You may assume He has no need for your services, but He does—so remain faithful. Gatekeepers don't get the glory, but they observe glory. Your gatekeeping gives you access to intimacy and wisdom. Enjoy your private conferences with Christ. You are loved when Jesus speaks your name. Stay near God's gate and you'll experience Him. You get to God as His gatekeeper!

"The gatekeeper opens the gate for him, and the sheep listen to his voice. He calls his own sheep by name and leads them out" (John 10:3).

How is Jesus my gate to God? What does it mean to be God's gatekeeper?

Related Readings
Numbers 16:26; Psalms 65:4; 84:2; 1 Chronicles 9:20-26; Luke 19:12-27

70

Peace Promise

———— ❧ ————

I will listen to what the LORD says;
he promises peace to his people, his faithful servants—
but let them not turn to folly.

PSALM 85:8

God promises peace to his people. It's a peace produced in heaven and delivered on earth. God's peace provides exactly what we need to excel in life, not just get by. The peace of God propels us to go places we would have avoided without the assurance of His peace. God's peace plan for His people is accessible at all times. It's when we forget to forge our faith around His plan that we forfeit peace.

God's peace process is to listen first and then act. Because God hears us, we're eager to hear Him. Hearing the voice of God vanquishes our fears and validates our peace. Grace waits to hear God, then proceeds in peace. The disciples waited on the peace of Jesus. The Spirit engulfed them, then they preached, performed miracles, and ministered to the people (John 20:21-23). God's peace proceeds from a heart of obedience. It's inaccessible to disobedience.

———— ❧ ————

"Therefore, since we have been justified through faith,
we have peace with God through our Lord Jesus Christ,
through whom we have gained access by faith into
this grace in which we now stand" (Romans 5:1-2).

Let the Lord in on your particular predicament. He already knows and cares. Confusion continues only when you try to work it out without Him. However, the peace of God doesn't require your total understanding. It transcends your troubled heart. It will guard your heart and mind in Christ Jesus (Philippians 4:7). Man's peace depends on treaties that can be broken. God's peace depends on your relationship with Jesus, which cannot be broken. Man's peace is momentary; God's peace is enduring.

Listen to man's voice and you may delay the peace process. Listen to God's voice and you'll accelerate the peace process. God provides peace to His children. His provision of His peace awaits your access. Therefore pray and wait on His peace. His peace precludes fear. Listen intently to the Lord. His voice can be trusted. Appropriate His peace promise.

In the middle of your storm, listen to His voice saying, "Peace, be still" (Mark 4:39 KJV). Calm comes with Christ.

What's the difference between Christ's peace and the world's peace? How can I apply God's peace to my life?

Related Readings
Isaiah 9:6; 52:7; Luke 1:79; 2:14; John 14:27; Ephesians 2:14,17

71

Undivided Heart

⸻◦◦◦⸻

Teach me your way, LORD,
that I may rely on your faithfulness;
give me an undivided heart,
that I may fear your name.

PSALM 86:11

An undivided heart unites around the will of God. The heart is headquarters for His purposes. It's here that humility reigns with focus and clarity, but pride's rule divides. The attributes of its scepter are awe and intimidation. Pride divides, while humility unites.

Our undivided devotion to God determines our other devotions, excluding some and creating others. As your faith becomes more focused, you become more focused. Perhaps this means you'll do fewer things well instead of many things poorly. Your life becomes a laser beam of implementation in the Lord's best. People may wonder why your efforts are increasingly intentional. You can tell them that God is teaching you to focus. Like an infant, you're growing beyond the milk of your salvation to the meat of His Word.

⸻◦◦◦⸻

"Let us move beyond the elementary teachings about
Christ and be taken forward to maturity" (Hebrews 6:1).

So an undivided heart is the Lord's student for life. There's no "arriving" in this life. We don't know it all until we're in the presence of the Almighty. The wise remain learners of the Lord's teachings.

An undivided heart craves teaching that goes beyond the surface of salvation to the depths of dependence on God. The mature understanding of God gets to the heart of the matter. It's in this place of integrity where you divide your heart in disobedience or unite it in obedience. An undivided heart places you on a path marked by His truth.

Avoid serving with a double mind. God hates double-mindedness (Psalm 119:113). Only when you draw near to God can you deal with double-mindedness (James 4:8). Unite your mind and heart around Christ and His teachings. Make His behavior the baseline for your life and work. It may mean relocating to a church that clearly teaches God's Word. It may mean breaking off a relationship that divides your heart and conflicts your mind. A united heart doesn't avoid the difficult path of obedience. It submits to its Savior and models Him.

"Come near to God and he will come near to you. Wash your hands, you sinners, and purify your hearts, you double-minded" (James 4:8).

What can I let go of and trust God with? Where do I need humility, so I can unite and not divide?

Related Readings
2 Chronicles 30:12; Ezekiel 11:19; Ephesians 4:3; Colossians 3:14; James 1:8

72

Faithful Foundation

⸺ ∞ ⸺

He has founded his city on the holy mountain.

PSALM 87:1

Your heavenly Father provides a faithful foundation. He provides it in your personal faith. When you placed your faith in Christ, you established your values and beliefs on the Rock of Ages. Faith is foundational for the character of Christ to transform your life. No amount of adversity or acclaim can remove His faithful foundation of holiness, humility, forgiveness, courage, and perseverance. Dismay dissolves when you place your trust in Christ. He's the cornerstone of your Sovereign Lord's foundation (Isaiah 28:16).

The church is established and built on the faithful foundation of Jesus. God's household is built on the foundation of the apostles and prophets with Christ as the chief cornerstone. In Him the whole building rises up to become His holy place of worship. The church of the living God is the pillar and foundation of truth.

⸺ ∞ ⸺

"You are…his household, built on the foundation
of the apostles and prophets, with Christ Jesus
himself as the chief cornerstone. In him the whole
building is joined together and rises to become
a holy temple in the Lord" (Ephesians 2:19-21).

The church is effective only as it implements its operational manual, the Bible. Christians can define truth only as it's taught from holy writ.

Full disclosure of God's Word invites the Holy Spirit's application to humble hearts. Stay engaged in a church whose foundation is faith in Christ, and whose pillars are the proclamation of Scripture. Hell cannot prevail against the church (Matthew 16:18).

Christians are called to devotion to one another. They honor one another above themselves (Romans 12:10). This level of relational unselfishness can only be founded on the Lord. Build on His foundation, and lay up for yourselves eternal rewards; you'll one day return to worship at His feet (Romans 4:11). Your faith, your church, and your relationships will flourish on God's faithful foundation. Become a bold builder on His pillar of truth!

"You will know how people ought to conduct themselves in God's household, which is the church of the living God, the pillar and foundation of the truth" (1 Timothy 3:15).

Is the foundation of my faith built on Christ? What truth does my conduct need to conform to?

Related Readings
1 Samuel 2:8; 1 Corinthians 3:10; Hebrews 11:10; Revelation 21:14

73

Afterlife

❦

Do you show your wonders to the dead?
Do those who are dead rise up and praise you?
PSALM 88:10

The afterlife is with the Lord for those who love Him; the afterlife is without the Lord for those who don't. This is why it's imperative that you get into right relationship with God in this life—so you don't get it wrong in eternity.

Yes, there's more to look forward to than cold dirt for your cold body. There's an afterlife. The dead in Christ shall rise first (1 Thessalonians 4:15-17). The same God who raised His Son Jesus will raise His sons and daughters in the faith. Take heart—a massive transformation will take place after this life. Advanced technology can prolong life, but it cannot resurrect life. No amount of discoveries will ever lead to that which is only in the hands of heaven. No amount of medicine can make a man or woman live forever. Death isn't bad for believers in Jesus Christ; it's a bridge of belief to something much better.

❦

"About the resurrection of the dead—have you not read what God said to you, 'I am the God of Abraham, the God of Isaac, and the God of Jacob'? He is not the God of the dead but of the living" (Matthew 22:31-32).

Take hope and live as if you'll one day rise from the dead. Life for those who love the Lord is not the dead-end street of sin, but a bridge into paradise with Jesus (Luke 23:43). You have the promise of your personal resurrection. You have the proof of your Savior's resurrection. Men and women who reject the resurrection route trod down the path to hell (Matthew 10:28; 2 Thessalonians 1:8-9; Revelation 20:11-15).

Existence without an afterlife is meaningless. By believing in an afterlife, we find this life full of purpose and eternal reward. This life is all about loving the Lord and loving people. This life is about dying to self and living for Him. This life is about gratitude and generosity, because of your gracious and gigantic God. The anticipation of an afterlife makes this life explode with meaning and hope. Be encouraged; you serve the God of the living!

—∞∞∞—

"He is the living God
and he endures forever;
his kingdom will not be destroyed,
his dominion will never end" (Daniel 6:26).

Am I ready for life after death? How can I live better in this life for the life to come?

Related Readings

Matthew 16:16; Acts 10:42; 1 Thessalonians 1:9; Hebrews 9:14

74

Secret Sins

You have set our iniquities before you,
our secret sins in the light of your presence.

PSALM 90:8

Secret sins do not remain secret. They're always before Almighty God, and they eventually come to light to those who love and respect us. Secret sins are risks that aren't worth taking. There's no upside, but there is a massive downside. Secret sins can seem harmless, but they're sinister in their intent and deadly in their outcome. Nothing good comes from secret sin. It leads to death. Death of life and relationships. Death of vision. Secret sins are spiritual suicide.

God's white-hot heart of love exposes sin. "God is light; in him is no darkness at all" (1 John 1:5). There are no secret sins before the Lord. He deals severely and justly with sin. But He did provide His Son Jesus as our Savior from secret sins. Without Jesus we cannot overcome sin's snare. A desire may feel good, but it can take control and give birth to sin. Sin produces death.

"When a person is carried away with desire and lured
by lust, and when desire becomes the focus and takes
control, it gives birth to sin. When sin becomes fully
grown, it produces death" (James 1:14-15 VOICE).

Fear God, and you'll fear sin. Fear of God fosters a healthy view of sin. The Lord loathes sin (Psalm 5:4-5), but He forgives the sinner

(1 John 1:9). Secret sin is cancer to your soul. It clutters your conscience. In Christ, however, you've been set free from sin and become a slave of God (Romans 6:22). The most effective remedy for secret sin is confession, repentance, and accountability.

Tell your spouse if you're emotionally attracted to a work associate. Don't keep secrets from those who hold you accountable. Admission can create a way out. Come out of the closet of compromise and come clean with Christ. Secluded sin gains control. Confessed sin loses control. Christ died openly for your concealed sin. Gratefully receive His public payment of your secret sin. Secret sin slithers away forgiven under the shadow of the cross. Don't keep sin a secret!

What concealed sin of mine has the Holy Spirit revealed? To whom do I need to confess my sin?

Related Readings
Psalm 7:14; Romans 6:23; Galatians 6:7; 1 Thessalonians 2:16

75

Rest in the Lord

———— ⊙◊⊙ ————

Whoever dwells in the shelter of the Most High
will rest in the shadow of the Almighty.

PSALM 91:1

The shadow of God is your shelter. He's your resting place. Resting in God's care produces peace. The wicked forfeit this peace (Isaiah 57:21).

We're tempted to run to our Savior's shelter only in times of trouble. Instead, we're to hang out habitually in God's inner sanctuary of intimacy.

Don't wait for hell to drive you to heaven. The Lord is not a last resort. He deserves and expects your full attention. Consequently, you get to reside in the peaceful presence of Jesus.

Rest is the fruit of remaining in Christ (John 15:4). When you're far from fellowship with your heavenly Father, you fret and find yourself fatigued. But when you're governed by grace, you obtain continual communion with Christ. Intimacy with Him offers rest.

———— ⊙◊⊙ ————

"Peace I [Jesus] leave with you; my
peace I give you" (John 14:27).

Make sure you don't substitute your devotion to God with your service for God. You rest only when your "Martha service" is motivated by your "Mary devotion" (Luke 10:38-42). Otherwise you become exhausted, ungrateful, and discouraged. Rest results from resting in

Him. So seek the shadow of the Almighty during the noxious heat of everyday life. Take one lunch break a week just to be with the Lord. Take a walk in the woods, or sit in the car and worship Him with uplifting music. Shut your office door and pray on your knees.

Take a deep breath of belief. You rest when you exhale worry and inhale trust. Under His reassuring shadow, you see Him. Take your attention off your struggles and fears. Focus on Him. Face God first; then you're ready to face your fears. The shadow of the Almighty is your security against insecurity. Your giants of fear become pygmies of peace when you rest under the influence of God's presence. Take shelter under His shadow. Rest under the Almighty.

"Because you are my help,
I sing in the shadow of your wings" (Psalm 63:7).

Have I run ahead of the Holy Spirit in my service? Is my unbelief keeping me from God's rest?

Related Readings
Psalm 7:14; Romans 6:23; Galatians 6:7; 1 Thessalonians 2:16

76

Stay Fresh

———⚬⚭⚬———

They will still bear fruit in old age,
they will stay fresh and green.

PSALM 92:14

Stay fresh in your faith. Otherwise you're set up to falter and not finish well. Fresh faith is compelling. It's clean and crisp like the beginning of a new day. But be aware: The older you get, the more familiar your faith becomes. It's easy to lose your freshness. Your focus drifts to your ailments and away from Almighty God. Your faith grows stale and tasteless. But fresh faith is appetizing and inviting. It piques the interest of others. They smell the aroma of your faith, and it's sweet to their senses.

Freshness comes by staying whole with God. Wholeness comes by your life becoming a garden of God's grace. Natural gardens decay, but a seasoned spiritual life bears much fruit. Keep the weeds out so you're positioned to finish well with a fresh and fruitful faith. Middle age and old age aren't for complaining, but for proclaiming the goodness of God. Like a freshly lit scented candle, your life has a pleasant scent. You are spiritually attractive.

———⚬⚭⚬———

"We are to God the pleasing aroma of Christ among those who are being saved and those who are perishing. To the one we are an aroma that brings death; to the other, an aroma that brings life. And who is equal to such a task?" (2 Corinthians 2:15-16).

The effects of staying fresh are compounding. Over time the outward man decays, but the inner man grows strong. God's work of grace keeps you fresh. He preserves believers to the end. Though declining, you're climbing higher and higher with Christ. Stay fresh by submitting to your Savior. Stay fresh by feeding your soul fresh bread from the Bible.

Stay fresh by investing in those who have yet to taste the grace of God. Stay fresh by trying new things and being around new believers. Stay fresh as a student of God and people. Fresh faith flourishes in fruit bearing. Make aging your ally, as freshness keeps you young at heart and keen in mind. Aged believers possess ripe experiences and a track record of God's trustworthiness. So stay fresh in your faith. Keep your garden of grace growing by the watering of the Word.

"That person is like a tree planted by streams of water, which yields its fruit in season" (Psalm 1:3).

How can I keep my faith fresh and fruitful? What are the advantages of getting older in the faith?

Related Readings

Psalm 52:8; Jeremiah 11:16; Ezekiel 47:12; John 15:2; 2 Corinthians 4:16-17

77

Tenacious Truth

Your statutes, LORD, stand firm;
holiness adorns your house
for endless days.

PSALM 93:5

The statutes of God stand firm forever. No secular storm can blow His truth from its moorings. No tempest of deceptive lies can untether truth from Almighty God. As the rocks remain unmoved from the tumult of the raging seas, so God's truth resists the shifting current of culture's opinions. Our faith is founded on the foundation of God's character. What He says can be trusted and acted upon, because He's 100 percent trustworthy.

Thank God for the outcome of His truth. His truth sets you free (John 8:32). His truth protects you (Psalm 40:11). His truth guides you (Psalm 25:5). His truth allows you to persevere (Proverbs 12:19). His truth creates value (Proverbs 16:13). His truth facilitates our worship (John 4:24). His truth is to be obeyed (Galatians 5:7). Knowing His truth leads to thanksgiving (1 Timothy 4:3). His truth brings joy (3 John 4).

"They perish because they refused to love the
truth and so be saved" (2 Thessalonians 2:10).

You can be extremely grateful to God for the fruit of His truth. Don't take truth for granted, but remain grateful instead. Remain a student of truth. This sends a signal of what you value and appreciate. The truth of God is a tremendous asset. Thank God for His truth. Praise the Lord for His precepts. His statutes stand firm. Let the truth of Almighty God transform your mind and heart. Be transformed by the renewing of your mind (Romans 12:2).

Keep your mind tidy with truth. Otherwise your mind becomes cluttered and confused with messy thinking. Invite Christ's truth to clean up the home of your heart. Then your heart will be furnished with the fixtures of His truth. Holiness will adorn your character and life. Right thinking and pure living are the goals of understanding and applying knowledge and truth.

Allow your pride to deflate and your humility to inflate under the influence of God's truth. Tenacious truth is your true north. Bend toward truth. Embrace truth. Believe and obey truth.

How is truth tied to the Lord's holiness? What truth do I need to embrace for God's Spirit to transform me?

Related Readings
Proverbs 4:6; Acts 28:25; Romans 9:1; Ephesians 1:13; 3 John 3

78

Christ's Consolation

*When anxiety was great within me,
your consolation brought me joy.*

PSALM 94:19

Anxiety can overwhelm us, like an imposing mountain too high to climb. It can drown us like an ocean riptide. An anxious heart is impossible to handle alone. It will continue to eat away at your peace and security until you're totally consumed by fear and failure. Anxiety kills relationships, because there's nothing left to give. Your emotional capacity is dried up with worry.

No one is immune to anxiety, but people tend to avoid the anxious. They feel preyed upon. Perpetual anxiety becomes relational dead weight. Sometimes worry attacks you from the rear in a relationship. You believe things are going just fine, then everything blows up in your face. You feel rejected and totally out of control. This is your time to refrain from attacking back, and instead to retreat with Christ. Replace anxiety and anger with trust and patience. Patience follows love. You're patient with who and what you love. Love is patient (1 Corinthians 13:4).

"Anxiety weighs down the heart,
but a kind word cheers it up" (Proverbs 12:25).

Allow the Lord to love you so you can love others. Christ is your counselor. He replaces your hurt with forgiveness. He transforms your sorrow with hope. He leads you out of rejection and into His sanctuary of rest. The counsel of Christ brings joy to your soul. The joy of Jesus is your jumping-off point in prayer. The comfort of Christ generates joy. Your extreme anxiety is God's opportunity. Your comfort flows out of communion with Christ. Soon you'll say goodbye to anxious thinking and replace it with joyful trust. Peace and gladness become giddy with God.

Christ consoles you so you can console others. You're a conduit for God's grace. Don't strive anxiously. Instead, go to God for grace and dispense it liberally. An ounce of grace is weightier than a ton of anxiety. "Do not be anxious about anything" (Philippians 4:6). Leave it with the Lord, and receive the joy of the Lord. He's your soul's strength and security!

How can I rest in Christ's consolation? Who needs to hear a word of comfort from me?

Related Readings

Job 6:10; 15:11; Ecclesiastes 11:10; 2 Corinthians 13:14; Philippians 2:1-4

79

Heart Issues

⟶ ∞ ⟵

Today, if only you would hear his voice,
"Do not harden your hearts as you did at Meribah,
as you did that day at Massah in the wilderness."

PSALM 95:7-8

A hardened heart cannot hear because it chooses not to listen. A crusty heart is obstinately ignorant to the ways of God. Its mind is made up to meander down the path of pride. A hardened heart wanders the wrong way (Hebrews 3:7-10). It's also hurtful, inflicting pain on itself and others. A hardened heart fossilizes faith. It builds up layers of hurt that encrust into stubbornness over time. It's trapped in a web of mistrust and misdeeds.

Humans harden hearts, and only heaven can soften them. It's the tender touch of Jesus that melts a man's heart. His love lubricates. He infuses humility—the cure for a hardened heart. A humble heart moves from a stubborn soul to a sensitive spirit. It grows from immaturity to maturity. It migrates from going its own way to following God's way. Humility softens hardness with healing. Mercy is liquid love. It saturates the dry clay of a crusty heart.

⟶ ∞ ⟵

"What does the LORD require of you?
To act justly and to love mercy
and to walk humbly with your God" (Micah 6:8).

The Lord is the potter and you are the clay. Clay humbly submits to its creator (Isaiah 29:16). Humility keeps you moldable and use-able. Otherwise, pride cracks under pressure. It becomes brittle and loses its boldness. Humility positions you to become the artwork of Almighty God.

Humble yourself under the mighty hand of God (1 Peter 5:6). Do it today in preparation for tomorrow. Pride procrastinates. Humility activates.

Your humility will ratchet up your capacity for listening. Then you can listen large. Listen to the Lord's voracious voice of wisdom. Listen to your caring spouse's voice of concern. Listen to your mentor's mature voice warning and reminding. Listen quietly to your humbled heart. Christ is calling you. He's the Shepherd of your sheep-like soul. Be bold, but loving. Be courageous, but caring. A humble heart hears and obeys the Lord.

"Because your heart was responsive and you humbled yourself before the Lord when you heard what I have spoken…and because you tore your robes and wept in my presence, I also have heard you, declares the Lord" (2 Kings 22:19).

Am I humble and teachable? In what area of my life do I need to humble myself before the Lord?

Related Readings
Exodus 10:3; Isaiah 57:15; Zechariah 7:9-10; Matthew 9:13; Acts 28:27

80

His Holiness

⚬⚬⚬

Worship the LORD in the splendor of his holiness;
tremble before him, all the earth.

PSALM 96:9

Holiness is the glorious combination of God's attributes. It sums up His comprehensive character. His wonder is overwhelming. God's holiness is a majestic sight to behold. Pure perfection is the splendor of the Lord. His holiness deserves our praise. In our humble worship we appreciate the Almighty for who He is: our awesome God—forever high and lifted up.

Some kings are deposed, and all eventually die, but our King reigns forever. His eternal throne towers above man's temporary monarchs. His holiness is regal, yet raw in reality. As we perceive the enormity of His holiness, we pray and worship in profound awe of the Almighty. If earthly kings engage our respect and honor, how much more should the King of kings? John felt this on the isle of Patmos. He describes the surreal effect of heaven's holiness on a mere human being.

⚬⚬⚬

"When I saw him, I fell at his feet as though
dead. Then he placed his right hand on me and
said: 'Do not be afraid. I am the First and the
Last. I am the Living One; I was dead, and behold
I am alive for ever and ever! And I hold the keys
of death and Hades'" (Revelation 1:17-18).

God's holiness adjusts our posture. It alters our lives. So ascribe to

Almighty God the glory due His name. Speak the Lord's name with holy reverence and fear. Do not speak of God glibly. Allow His holiness to make your character attractive. It's in the presence of Holy God that you're convicted of unholy attitudes, actions, and conversations. Look into His loving eyes and allow Him to create a countenance of compassion on your face. Be holy as He is holy (1 Peter 1:15-16).

Without the grace of God, we're ugly and untethered. However, the Holy Spirit surprises us with heart beautification. He executes an extreme makeover of our soul and spirit. Our life is made lovely under the transforming power of Holy God. His holiness is our asset of attractiveness. Behold His beauty, and grow beautiful. Worship the Lord in the splendor of His holiness!

"I saw the Lord, high and exalted, seated on a throne; and the train of his robe filled the temple" (Isaiah 6:1).

How can I worship God in the beauty of His holiness? How does He want to purify my heart?

Related Readings
Exodus 23:25; Isaiah 35:8; Jonah 1:9; 1 Thessalonians 4:7; 1 John 3:3

81

Be Glad

The LORD reigns, let the earth be glad;
let the distant shores rejoice.

PSALM 97:1

Y ou can be glad because the Lord reigns. He reigns over the righteous and the unrighteous. God governs the universe. Christ is in control. Jesus said, "All authority in heaven and on earth has been given to me" (Matthew 28:18). These are comforting words to those of us who follow Christ. Only those who reject or forget Jesus recoil from His reign. They live in a sad state. But for us, there's great joy and comfort knowing Christ is on His throne. The reign of earthly rulers can be ruinous and unrighteous, but the reign of God gives life and righteousness. Be glad.

Your life may seem little right now. You feel faithless and overwhelmed by a barrage of disbelief, problems, and misconceptions. You may feel taken advantage of, lied about, or misunderstood. Your faith may be fractured under this unfair weight. Sadness is seeping into your soul.

Don't despair. Christ cares. He infuses joy into hard situations.

"Consider it pure joy, my brothers and sisters,
whenever you face trials of many kinds,
because you know that the testing of your faith
produces perseverance" (James 1:2-3).

There's good news. Your heavenly Father has not been deposed by the devil. Satan cannot usurp the authority of Almighty God. The kingdoms of this world are full of injustice, crime, and punishment. The kingdom of God is just, freeing, and rewarding. Bow in belief to King Jesus. He'll dispense hope and joy to your hurting heart. God gives gladness. Jesus prayed, "Your kingdom come, your will be done, on earth as it is in heaven" (Matthew 6:10).

God's will is that He reign in and through His saints. His followers are to engage as kingdom citizens. Be glad, for the day is coming when His people will reign exclusively over His kingdom. Be glad that you're not of this world, though you're in the world as His representative. Be glad you're God's. Be glad He reigns over life and death. Be glad He's your King!

———— ⊰∞⊱ ————

"The sovereignty, power and greatness of all the kingdoms under heaven will be handed over to the holy people of the Most High. His kingdom will be an everlasting kingdom, and all rulers will worship and obey him" (Daniel 7:27).

What's out of my control that I can entrust to Christ's control? Is the joy of Jesus my strength?

Related Readings
Psalm 9:2; Matthew 5:12; Acts 5:41; 2 Corinthians 6:10; Hebrews 10:34

82

Be Joyful

———— ⊗⊗⊙ ————

Let the rivers clap their hands,
let the mountains sing together for joy;
*let them sing before the L*ORD,
for he comes to judge the earth.

PSALM 98:8-9

Almighty God's judgment is accompanied by the joy of His handiwork. Celebrate Christ's coming! Celebrate His first coming, for He has done marvelous things. His life was matchless in pure virtue. His death was sacrificial in providing salvation for all who believe. His resurrection was electric in releasing eternal energy for all who are filled by His Holy Spirit. You can rejoice because of the righteous judgment of God. Joyful surrender readies you for Christ's coming.

Mary understood joy at the first coming of Jesus. After the angel's words sunk in that she was to become a mom, the mother of God, she exclaimed, "My soul glorifies the Lord, and my spirit rejoices in God my Savior" (Luke 1:46-47). Becoming a mother encompassed her soul with joy. Baby Jesus was her joy. She couldn't keep quiet, for the coming of her Lord and her child was at hand. Joy resonated in the heavens and resounded throughout the earth.

———— ⊗⊗⊙ ————

"A woman giving birth to a child has pain because
her time has come; but when her baby is born
she forgets the anguish because of her joy that
a child is born into the world" (John 16:21).

Live your life in triumphant victory, not in dismal defeat. You are more than a conqueror through Christ, through Him who loves you (Romans 8:37). The Lord's great love is your life preserver. "The joy of the Lord is your strength" (Nehemiah 8:10). You serve a risen Savior who's in the world today. Make sure your security and significance are in Christ and not in your son or daughter. Your identity is in Christ. Go regularly to Jesus for a cup of joy. Drink often.

Don't allow mistreatment or inequity to rob your joy. God will one day judge with equity. His days seem longer than ours, so be patient. Turn off the depressing songs of Satan. He's a joy killer. Reject his joyless tunes. Instead, tune in to your trustworthy Savior Jesus. Sing at the top of your lungs to the Lord. Sing the new song Christ has composed. His Holy Spirit harmonizes your life with joy and peace. Sing joyfully for what He has done, is doing, and will do. Be joyful in Jesus!

"Sing for joy, you heavens, for the Lord has done this;
shout aloud, you earth beneath" (Isaiah 44:23).

How has Satan tried to steal my joy? What blessings from the Lord can I regularly rejoice about?

Related Readings
Psalms 68:3; 100:2; Habakkuk 3:18; Romans 12:12; Philippians 2:2; 4:1

83

Praying Leaders

—————— ⟡ ——————

Moses and Aaron were among his priests,
Samuel was among those who called on his name;
they called on the LORD
and he answered them.

PSALM 99:6

W hy do leaders need to pray? Prayer protects leaders from substituting their own accomplishments for God's favor. They're tempted to take matters into their own hands and forget heaven. They can drive so hard that they hinder the work of the Holy Spirit. Leaders are great candidates for prayer, because they're out front and exposed to the enemy. Prayer positions them for success.

They need prayer's protection. In distress the devil tempts them. In success, pride seduces them. Leaders need to look to the Lord, for He is their all-knowing leader. Paul, on the road to Damascus, was arrested by Almighty God's grace. Blinded by the light of God's leadership, he followed without fully knowing where it would take him (Acts 22:6-11). Leaders need prayer because God's plan is much bigger than the mind alone can comprehend. Prayer gives faith and hope.

—————— ⟡ ——————

"Be joyful in hope, patient in affliction,
faithful in prayer" (Romans 12:12).

Praying leaders have a profound impact on those around them. The residue of prayer rubs off on others: faith, hope, love, grace, forgiveness, purity, and courage. On bended knee you gain the wisdom, confidence, and creditability to stand and lead. Learning to lead comes out of the discipline of prayer. Prayer restrains you from racing ahead of the Lord. The disciples learned to rely on the Spirit's lead for a leadership need (Acts 1:12-14).

Praying leaders will magnify their utter dependence on God. You pray like you breathe, often and unconsciously. Invest the time to pray with and for your team. Prayer breathes life. It's your first offensive tactic, not your last resort. Prayer isn't your plan B—it's always plan A. Gather your family together to pray for the sick, the lost, and leaders in authority (1 Timothy 2:1-3). Pray when you feel led and when you don't. The effect of your prayers isn't based on your feelings, but on faith. Praying leaders see God—and see Him transform their lives!

—∞∞∞—

"The prayer of a righteous person is
powerful and effective" (James 5:16).

In what ways can my leadership be more dependent on God in prayer? Is my character keeping up with my success?

Related Readings
1 Kings 18:41-45; Matthew 7:7; Mark 1:35; John 9:31; Acts 20:36

84

Enduring Love

————— ∞ —————

*For the L*ORD *is good and his love endures forever;*
his faithfulness continues through all generations.

PSALM 100:5

The love of God never ceases. Christ's love is continual because it flows from the inexhaustible reservoir of God's goodness. Man's lakes may languish for lack of rain, but not the love of the Lord. There's no drought of love in the divine scheme of things. It rains down from heaven in massive sheets of mercy and faithfulness. It pelts our pride and melts our heart. The love of God endures. Your heavenly Father's love is not fickle. It is faithful and true.

Your earthly father's love may be conditional and undependable. It may be hard for him to love, because he's rarely been loved himself. But you have the opportunity and privilege of moving beyond the drought of your dad's love to bow beneath the waterfall of Christ's compassion. Christ's covenant of love with His children never falters. You can forever trust in God's unfailing love.

————— ∞ —————

"I am like an olive tree
flourishing in the house of God;
I trust in God's unfailing love
for ever and ever" (Psalm 52:8).

Because of God's enduring love, you have reason to rejoice. His love is your excuse to exercise continual praise and thanksgiving. Don't remain defeated by dire circumstances and negative thinking. God loves you. He has saved your soul. God loves you. He has made you whole. God loves you. He provides you work. God loves you. He has given you life. Your shouts of joy drown out the murmurings in your mind. You are His. "Owned by God" is your trademark of trust. Let gratitude govern your thinking, because God's love endures forever.

Because His love is everlasting, you have Christ's capacity to love continually. You can love sinners and saints alike. Jesus did (Luke 5:30). He spent time with people unlike Himself. This is the posture of love. Release God's love to shine through your soul. Be a leader in love. It's Christ's love, manifested through you, that the Lord uses to lead others to Himself. Be a lover who endures. Love in the good times and especially in the hard times. Love endures!

⊷⊶⊷

"Give thanks to the LORD,
for his love endures forever" (2 Chronicles 20:21).

How does God express His enduring love to me? What's my response to His love?

Related Readings
Psalm 138:8; Isaiah 55:3; Jeremiah 33:11; 1 Corinthians 8:3; James 1:12

85

Eye Protection

————— ∞ —————

I will conduct the affairs of my house
with a blameless heart.
I will not look with approval
on anything that is vile.
I hate what faithless people do;
I will have no part in it.

PSALM 101:2-3

Spiritual eyesight is a gift from God. His Spirit allows us to see and understand spiritual truths (1 Corinthians 2:12-14). This is why we want our walk with Christ to be blameless. A blameless life is able to behold Almighty God and His attributes. Your blameless life keeps your eyesight from becoming blurred to your Savior. You see the goodness of God above the wickedness of the world.

The object of your faith focus begins at home. Your heart needs the Spirit's eye protection from worldly media. Where your eyes give permission, the heart gives admission. Eve and Adam were first fixated by the appeal of the fruit to their eyes (Genesis 3:6-7). Their eyes were opened by sin to sin. Once its allure entered their eyes, it arrested their minds and hands. They ignored the protection of their eyes. Eye protection is essential to enjoying a close walk with Christ.

————— ∞ —————

"I made a solemn pact with myself never to
undress a girl with my eyes" (Job 31:1 MSG).

Don't flirt with sin; view it with scorn and abhorrence. Christ died for our sins (1 Corinthians 15:3); the least we can do is die to sin. By faith, Paul died daily (1 Corinthians 15:31). Abundant life (John 10:10) is preceded by ongoing death. The sirens of sin will seduce you more often than not. Avoid what you see coming. Flee from temptation. Eye protection is an invitation to walk with Christ.

Expose your eyes to what's acceptable to your heavenly Father. He's serious about how you steward your eyesight (Matthew 5:29). Your eyes are a paintbrush to the canvas of your soul. Use both of them to create works of art, pleasing to the Almighty. This inner artwork is attractive to those who love you the most. Nonetheless, be wise where you look. Look on God's creation with admiration and awe. Where you look is what you become—so be selective and protective with your eyes. Focus on the good. Have an eye for the eternal. Look to the Lord first and foremost!

―――∞∞∞―――

"Blessed are the pure in heart,
for they will see God" (Matthew 5:8).

What does it mean to see God? How can I protect my eyes from unseemly images?

Related Readings
Psalm 119:18; Hosea 9:10; John 6:46; 1 Corinthians 2:9

86

Cry for Help

〰️

Hear my prayer, LORD;
let my cry for help come to you.

PSALM 102:1

Sometimes you feel desperate. Your needs get the best of you, overwhelming you. Your sorrow has intensified your prayers into crying. But this is the design of distress. Pain is meant to drive you to God. You cry out to Christ because He cares. Seek heaven for help. Listening to Jesus provides resources for abundant living. In solitude a troubled soul can be soothed.

Trouble finds trust and peace in Christ (John 14:1-6). You find security with your Savior. A cry for help is humbling, but it's not meant to be humiliating. It's those who refuse help who look foolish. Wisdom cries out to God. It acknowledges the Almighty.

Seek often the kind face of your heavenly Father. Don't allow your inner woes, your personal enemies, or your physical ailments to drive a wedge between you and God. Prayer is a bridge to belief in Christ.

〰️

"Because Jesus lives forever...he is able to
save completely those who come to God
through him, because he always lives to
intercede for them" (Hebrews 7:25).

Pause in your painful lamentation and earnestly seek the Lord. Your complaint to Christ will not be held against you. Release your anger and receive God's grace. The person with whom you have conflict may never change, but you can. Receive God's love, so you can love. Receive God's forgiveness, so you can forgive. Receive Christ's courage, so you can be courageous. Receive the joy of Jesus, so you can be joyful. Receive heaven's hope, so you can be hopeful. There's weeping in the night, but joy comes in the morning (Psalm 30:5).

Sincere supplication to your Savior is your aggressive ally. Use it for yourself and others. Don't be shy about acquainting others with your grief. Don't struggle through life bearing your burdens alone (Galatians 6:2). Some will find a blessing in being your burden bearer. Christians are meant to live in community, not in the silent cries of isolation. The Lord listens to your cries. He cares. He loves. He has sent His Word to heal your wounded heart.

"He sent out his word and healed them;
he rescued them from the grave" (Psalm 107:20).

How does the Lord want to comfort your heart? Who else can carry your burden with you?

Related Readings
Exodus 2:23; Psalm 4:1; Isaiah 25:8; Luke 18:7; Hebrews 5:7

87

Benefits Package

⟿

Praise the L*ORD*, *my soul,*
and forget not all his benefits.

PSALM 103:2

God's benefits package is exceedingly generous. It's not limited to human resources, but embraces heaven's resources. He forgives your sins and gives you eternal life insurance. His sick leave includes healing from disease. He rescues you from the pit of purposeless living and places you in a caring community with convictions. He crowns you with love and compassion. He satisfies your longings with good things. He renews your energy, so you can engage life.

God's benefits to believers far exceed what we deserve. The Lord's presence is music to the ears of our soul. His comforting Spirit causes us to burst forth in praise, "Bless the Lord, O my soul." Our praise contains more gratitude to God than our tongues alone can tell.

Like Moses, you may be so inundated by His benefits you have to request relief from His blessings (Exodus 36:5-6). His bountiful benefits require wise management. Your great God is generous to provide.

⟿

"Command those who are rich in this present
world not to be arrogant nor to put their hope
in wealth, which is so uncertain, but to put
their hope in God, who richly provides us with
everything for our enjoyment" (1 Timothy 6:17).

Remember the spouse you prayed for and how God gave you much more than you deserved. You're the benefactor of a companion who cares for you like Christ. How beneficial is the job He has given you? It's probably not perfect, but it's perfect for you. Your job is a platform for kingdom influence. Steward, work well. Serve unselfishly. His benefits are a treasure entrusted to you. Use His benefits to you for the benefit of others.

Christ's benefits to His followers are bold and life-changing. His benefits package is superabundant. The Lord's favor exceeds the world's standards. His blessings of character make you a better person. You're meant to wear His attributes of holiness, love, forgiveness, mercy, compassion, and grace. Yes, from the depths of your soul, bless the Lord and forget not all His benefits!

∞

"Hope does not put us to shame, because God's love has been poured out into our hearts through the Holy Spirit, who has been given to us" (Romans 5:5).

How can I thank the Lord for His generous benefits? Who can I bless with God's rich blessings?

Related Readings
Nehemiah 4:14; Job 33:26; Psalm 25:6; Acts 20:35; Ephesians 1:3

88

Gladden the Heart

*He makes grass grow for the cattle,
and plants for people to cultivate—
bringing forth food from the earth:
wine that gladdens human hearts,
oil to make their faces shine,
and bread that sustains their hearts.*

PSALM 104:14-15

God meant for wine to gladden the heart. It originates from the fruit of His creation. Jesus made wine at the wedding of a friend (John 2:1-11). This was the first of His miracles that grew His disciples' faith in Him. Wine is for times of celebration and relational investment—not self-indulgence. Responsible consumption requires self-control. Wise use precludes foolishness.

Don't partake if it causes a brother or sister to stumble (Romans 14:21). Those who are mature never intentionally tempt others. The wise abstain in deference to those who abstain. Wine's design is to make the heart merry, but not to inebriate the mind. It's to be enjoyed in moderation, not in drunkenness. Instead, allow Christ to control your life through the filling of His Spirit.

"Do not get drunk on wine, which leads to debauchery.
Instead, be filled with the Spirit" (Ephesians 5:18).

Alcohol causes you to lose your inhibitions, and that can lead to unsavory behavior. This is why wisdom enjoys wine with accountability.

Don't drink if it leads you into temptation. The wise use of wine is limited, or none at all. Avoid its blessing becoming a curse. If you're a leader, be extremely cautious. One bad night can stain a lifetime of respected reputation. Wise use refrains.

Use your freedom to drink or not to drink with humility and sensitivity. In either case, you're not necessarily any more spiritual. Arrogance from not drinking wine is as ugly as drunkenness. When you're with those who believe differently, don't lord over them your freedom to abstain or not. God's good creation is not to be polluted by pride. As the Lord leads, enjoy the fruit of the vine. Allow God to gladden your heart through the wise use of wine. Be discreet. Be accountable. Be responsible. Be glad!

"Wine is a mocker and beer a brawler;
whoever is led astray by them is
not wise" (Proverbs 20:1).

How can I use my abstinence of alcohol to benefit others? Am I discreet and disciplined in my use of wine?

Related Readings

Genesis 9:21-23; 19:32-36; Numbers 6:1-4; John 2:1-11;
1 Timothy 3:8

89

Position of Influence

———⸎———

[Egypt's king] made [Joseph] master of his household,
ruler over all he possessed,
to instruct his princes as he pleased
and teach his elders wisdom.

PSALM 105:21-22

You're in a position of influence for a purpose. A significant part of your purpose is to influence influencers. Just as God raised up Joseph, He may have positioned you in a place you couldn't have scripted alone. He has taken your troubled circumstances and turned them into an opportunity for good. Because you were faithful during the stressful times, He has opened a door of influence. Pray for those around you, and invest your wisdom and time in them. Leaders need godly counselors they can trust (Proverbs 15:22).

Stay humble and teachable. Invite the Holy Spirit to engraft God's Word into your heart and mind. A growing soul gains influence over other seeking souls. You earn the right to be respected and followed as you submit to Almighty God and the authorities in your life. Joseph was falsely accused and mistreated, but he kept the high road of submission to the process until truth prevailed. He trusted God for equity and justice. Joseph's influence grew as he grew in faith.

———⸎———

"But Joseph said to them, 'Don't be afraid. Am I in the
place of God? You intended to harm me, but God

intended it for good to accomplish what is now being
done, the saving of many lives'" (Genesis 50:19-20).

Use your position of influence first and foremost to point people
to Christ. Start with the small circle of those who know you best, then
watch the Lord leverage your influence into a grander scale for His
glory. Authorities invite influence from those they trust. Stay trustworthy in the small things, and the larger ones will take care of themselves (Matthew 25:21).

See your influence as a stewardship. You invest in your children for
life when you regularly tell them, "I'm so proud of how God is using
you," or when you remark to your spouse, "I love you; you're God's
gift to me." Most of all, be influenced by Jesus. Hide His Word in
your heart (Psalm 119:11). Make prayer a priority. Listen to the Lord
and do what He says. The most effective influencers are those who are
influenced by Christ. Be a person of integrity, and your influence will
never lack the Lord's blessing. Your influence is God's gift to use for
His purposes.

"Do you see someone skilled in their work?
They will serve before kings" (Proverbs 22:29).

How can I use my influence for God's kingdom? How do I need
the Spirit to influence me?

Related Readings
Genesis 41:46; Exodus 18:19; 1 Kings 11:28; Acts 27:11;
1 Timothy 4:12

90

Consistent Behavior

⸻

*Blessed are those who act justly,
who always do what is right.*

PSALM 106:3

In the power of the Holy Spirit seek to do right as the Lord defines right. Consistent behavior brings out the blessing of God and incurs the favor of man. Yes, there will be those who snarl at your good works, but this is to be expected. Proud men punished Daniel because he did what was right with his persistent prayers (Daniel 6:10-12). Not everyone is interested in integrity, but most want to be treated right.

Better to constantly pray to Christ and receive clarity than to stay confused with inconsistent intercession. Constant prayer keeps you aware of the Almighty's agenda; it's your "check and balance" to good behavior. Be constantly in the presence of Christ and be conformed to the truth that you're wholly His. The Lord's ownership requires holiness—this brings happiness to a humble heart. Christ blesses a life aligned with His will.

⸻

"Blessed [anticipating God's presence, spiritually
mature] are the pure in heart [those with
integrity, moral courage, and godly character],
for they will see God" (Matthew 5:8 AMP).

Constantly do right, and you'll grow the equity of your integrity. Consistent character gives you creditability, respect, and influence.

For instance, follow through with your word, especially when circumstances change. If you quoted someone a sale price or made a generous promise to a friend, follow through—even though the facts may have shifted out of your favor. Relationships are more important than money. Your consistent behavior may be what wins others to Christ.

Define and do right as outlined by Almighty God. Christ's concordance of right is laid out in His Holy Word. "It is written" (Matthew 4:4) was a constant phrase that seasoned the lips of Jesus. In teaching and conversation He quoted Scripture because it was His baseline for belief and behavior. Adhere to the Almighty's words, and you'll effectively do His work. Constantly doing right isn't always fun, but it's freeing when you look into the face of Jesus with no regrets. By God's grace, constantly do what's right, and people will see Jesus in you.

"Let your light shine before others, that
they may see your good deeds and glorify
your Father in heaven" (Matthew 5:16).

Is my behavior consistent with Christ's expectations? Where is Jesus calling me to more consistency?

Related Readings
Proverbs 8:30; Acts 1:14; Hebrews 5:14; James 1:7-8

How to Become
a Disciple of Jesus Christ

Jesus came to them and said, "All authority in heaven and on earth has been given to me. Therefore go and make disciples of all nations, baptizing them in the name of the Father and of the Son and of the Holy Spirit, and teaching them to obey everything I have commanded you. And surely I am with you always, to the very end of the age."

MATTHEW 28:18-20

Holy Scripture provides principles regarding becoming a disciple and making disciples:

Believe

Belief in Jesus Christ as your Savior and Lord gives you eternal life in heaven.

> If you declare with your mouth, "Jesus is Lord," and believe in your heart that God raised him from the dead, you will be saved (Romans 10:9).

Repent and Be Baptized

To repent is to turn from your sin and to publicly confess Christ in baptism.

> Repent and be baptized, every one of you, in the name of Jesus Christ for the forgiveness of your sins. And you will receive the gift of the Holy Spirit (Acts 2:38).

Obey

Obedience is an indicator of our love for the Lord Jesus and His presence in our life.

> Jesus replied, "Anyone who loves me will obey my teaching. My Father will love them, and we will come to them and make our home with them" (John 14:23).

Worship, Prayer, Community, Evangelism, and Study

Worship and prayer express our gratitude and honor to God and our dependence on His grace. Community and evangelism show our accountability to Christians and compassion for non-Christians. Study to apply the knowledge, understanding, and wisdom of God.

> Every day they continued to meet together in the temple courts. They broke bread in their homes and ate together with glad and sincere hearts, praising God and enjoying the favor of all the people. And the Lord added to their number daily those who were being saved (Acts 2:46-47).

Love God

Intimacy with Almighty God is a growing and loving relationship. We're loved by Him so that we can love others and be empowered by the Holy Spirit to obey His commands.

> Jesus replied: "'Love the Lord your God with all your heart and with all your soul and with all your mind.' This is the first and greatest commandment" (Matthew 22:37-38).

Love People

Our love for others flows from our love for our heavenly Father. We're able to love because He first loved us.

> And the second is like it: "Love your neighbor as yourself" (Matthew 22:39).

Make Disciples

We disciple others because we're grateful to God and to those who disciple us, and because we want to obey Christ's last instructions before going to heaven.

> The things you have heard me say in the presence of many witnesses entrust to reliable people who will also be qualified to teach others (2 Timothy 2:2).

About the Author

Boyd Bailey enjoys the role of chief encouragement officer at Ministry Ventures, a company he cofounded in 1999. His passion is to encourage and equip leaders engaged in kingdom-focused enterprises. Since 2004 he has also served as president and founder of Wisdom Hunters, a ministry that connects people to Christ through devotional writing—with more than 100,000 daily email readers.

Ministry Ventures has trained approximately 1000 faith-based nonprofits and has coached for certification more than 200 ministries in the best practices of prayer, board development, ministry model, administration, and fundraising. By God's grace, these ministries have raised more than $100 million, and thousands of people have been led into growing relationships with Jesus Christ.

Prior to the founding of Ministry Ventures, Boyd was the national director for Crown Financial Ministries. He was instrumental in the expansion of Crown into 30 major markets across the United States. He was a key facilitator in the $25 million merger between Christian Financial Concepts and Crown Ministries.

Before his work with Crown, Boyd and Andy Stanley started First Baptist Atlanta's north campus, and as an elder, Boyd assisted Andy in the start of North Point Community Church.

Boyd received a bachelor of arts degree from Jacksonville State University and a masters of divinity degree from Southwestern Seminary in Fort Worth, Texas. Boyd and his wife, Rita, live in Roswell, Georgia. They've been married 35 years and are blessed with four daughters, three sons-in-law, and five grandchildren.

Also from Boyd Bailey

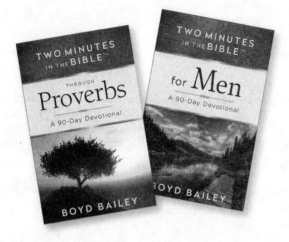

To learn more about Harvest House books or
to read sample chapters, visit our website:

www.harvesthousepublishers.com

HARVEST HOUSE PUBLISHERS
EUGENE, OREGON